VGM Opportunities Series

OPPORTUNITIES IN
SOCIAL SCIENCE
CAREERS

Rosanne J. Marek

Foreword by
John E. Weakland
Editor
International Journal of Social Education

VGM Career Horizons
a division of *NTC Publishing Group*
Lincolnwood

Cover Photo Credits:

Upper left courtesy of American Anthropological Association, Arlington, Virginia.
Reprinted by permission of M. Yasar Iscan.
Upper right courtesy of Rand McNally/William Franklin McMahon.
Lower left photo by K. C. Smith. Courtesy the Museum of Florida History,
Tallahassee, Florida.
Lower right courtesy of International Business Machines Corporation.
Unauthorized use not permitted.

Library of Congress Cataloging-in-Publication Data

Marek, Rosanne J.
    Opportunities in social science careers / Rosanne J. Marek. —
Rev. ed.
        p.   cm. — (VGM opportunities series)
    Includes bibliographical references.
    ISBN 0-8442-4573-9 (alk. paper). — ISBN
0-8442-4574-7 (pbk. : alk. paper)
        1. Social sciences—Vocational guidance—United States.
I. Title.   II. Series.
H62.5.U5M37   1997
300'.23'73—dc21   96-47281
                                                            CIP

Published by VGM Career Horizons, a division of NTC Publishing Group
4255 West Touhy Avenue
Lincolnwood (Chicago), Illinois 60646-1975, U.S.A.
© 1997 by NTC Publishing Group. All rights reserved.
No part of this book may be reproduced, stored in a retrieval
system, or transmitted in any form or by any means,
electronic, mechanical, photocopying, recording or otherwise,
without the prior permission of NTC Publishing Group.
Manufactured in the United States of America.

7 8 9 0 VP 9 8 7 6 5 4 3 2 1

CONTENTS

Preparing for a career in psychology. Sources of
additional information.

salaries. Teacher supply and demand. High school
preparation. Teaching the social sciences in colleges
and universities. Sources of additional information.

Overview of the social sciences. Career/Prerequisites.
Careers and the social sciences. Choosing a college or
university. Conclusion.

ABOUT THE AUTHOR

Rosanne J. Marek is chair of the Department of History at Ball State University in Muncie, Indiana. She received her doctorate from Kent State University and her master of science degree from the University of Dayton. She teaches undergraduate students in survey courses in American and world history and preservice social studies teachers. Prior to coming to Ball State, she taught in several elementary schools in Ohio.

For several years Dr. Marek worked with Ball State students who had not yet selected a major. She established the university's Learning Center and served as its director for two years.

She is a past president of the Indiana Association for Developmental Education and a member of the Awards Committee of the National Council for the Social Studies. She is a member of several organizations including the Organization of American Historians, the Indiana Council for the Social Studies, the National Council for History Education, the National Council for Geographic Education, and the American Historical Association.

ACKNOWLEDGMENTS

The assistance of several persons in the completion of this book is gratefully acknowledged. Chief among them are Joan Ouano Erasga, who compiled much of the data for this revised edition; Jack E. Ihle, a psychologist at the university's Counseling and Psychological Services Center; the Career Services staff at Ball State University, especially Mridula Jarial, coordinator of its Resource Center; and Ellen Urban, who edited this revision.

FOREWORD

Since the emergence of civilization over five millennia ago, thoughtful people of every era have proposed various social theories to explain the relationship between human beings and society; however, the social sciences are relatively new. In the aftermath of the Age of Reason, the methods of physical science came to be applied to disparate disciplines, some of which were of ancient origin and others new upon the scene in the nineteenth century. These disciplines, which deal with aspects of society or forms of social activity, we call the social sciences. As Rosanne J. Marek points out, "it is the social sciences that enable us to look beyond facts to values." Furthermore, "it is they that encourage us to aspire to knowledge and ultimately to wisdom." These disciplines include anthropology, sociology, psychology, history, geography, political science, and economics, all of which are discussed in this very useful book, together with a chapter on teaching and the social sciences.

In these difficult times, students need as much assistance as possible in choosing a career and finding a job. In this revised edition of *Opportunities in Social Science Careers,* Rosanne J. Marek provides this help by succinctly describing each discipline and discussing employment opportunities, salaries, and educational requirements for each field. Each chapter also includes a list of organizations to which students can write for additional information. Included in this revised edition are Canadian professional organizations and certification offices as well. The concluding chapter offers an excellent overview of careers in the social sciences, careers that can be extremely fulfilling. As Dr. Marek notes, those who choose such careers "are, after all, striving to be truly human." This is the great task of us all, and there can be no greater satisfaction.

John E. Weakland, Editor
*International Journal of
Social Education*

DEDICATION

To my parents, Helen and James F. Marek, who taught me that life involves far more than just earning a living; to my sisters, Cecile and Jane, who are also my dearest friends; and to my nephews, Michael and Ian, who have shown me how joyous aunthood can be.

CHAPTER 1

CAREERS IN THE NEXT CENTURY

COMPETENCIES FOR SUCCESS

In an address in Ashland, Kentucky, in late August of 1996, President Bill Clinton observed that in five years the youth of today will have job opportunities that currently don't exist. Indeed, there are jobs today that were unheard of a decade ago. The technology explosion has changed the world of work. Some skills, competencies, and proficiencies needed today differ vastly from those of an earlier time. This fact, coupled with the reality that most college students of the nineties will change careers an estimated seven times during their lifetimes, requires the development of transferable skills such as planning, organizing, analyzing, and evaluating.

Academic competencies or broad intellectual skills are essential to work effectively in all fields of study. Simply, they are basic for success in college. Knowledge of what is expected is crucial to effective learning. In 1983 the College Board published an excellent booklet, *Academic Preparation for College: What Students Need to Know and Be Able to Do*. Though written more than thirteen years ago, much of its content is applicable today. In its discussion of the competencies needed for success, the College Board states that because we live in a distinct kind of society, all people need to understand how modern societies function and how they developed. People need information concerning past civilizations and their links to present ones. If people are to perform effectively as citizens in a democratic society, they need knowledge about central institutions and values in their own society as well as in other major societies around the world. They also need to comprehend the global context of contemporary life.

Defining problems and employing various kinds of information in seeking solutions to those problems require the analytical skills acquired in the study of the social sciences. Knowledge of computers is basic to understanding the full range of procedures that may be applied to organizing information and solving problems in the social sciences. For all the careers outlined in this book, a knowledge of computer technology is needed. People considering careers in the social sciences should have a basic knowledge of how computers work and an understanding of common computer terminology. They should be able to use appropriate software for the collection and retrieval of information and for word processing, modeling, working with simulations, and decision-making. They also must have some understanding of the problems and issues confronting us in the use of computers, including their social and economic effects on our lives and the ethics involved in their use.

CHAPTER 2

WHAT ARE THE SOCIAL SCIENCES?

In 1967, Lyndon Johnson, who was president at the time, wrote that excellence in human endeavors can flow only from the quality of the society and the good fortune of the nation. He later said that our country was very much in need of clear eyes and stout hearts. America, according to Johnson, had proved its scientific and technical genius. Its citizens, however, seemed to lack the vision and courage to improve the human condition.

Scientific technology, as someone has said, has taught us to fly higher and faster than birds and to swim deeper and farther than fish, but it has not taught us to walk the earth as rational, human beings. In other words, while technology can give us the goods we need to make life more comfortable, the humanities and social sciences must give us the goals we need to make life more worthwhile.

For it is the social sciences that enable us to look beyond facts to values. It is they that encourage us to aspire to knowledge and ultimately to wisdom. In understanding the social sciences, we realize that learning exists not for its own sake but rather for the sake of all humankind.

The focus of this book is on career opportunities in the social sciences. Seven fields of study—history, geography, economics, political science, sociology, anthropology, and psychology—are recognized as the social sciences. Although they differ from each other in their purpose and scope, they share one essential component. Each studies individuals and their relationship with each other and their environment. Indeed, the Latin origins of the term *social sciences* can be translated as knowledge about human beings as companions, that is, social beings.

THE BROAD SCOPE OF SOCIAL SCIENCES

The total human experience is the source of content for the social sciences. In the following chapters, each of the seven disciplines will be examined. Selected careers in each field will be identified. Information concerning the training and education required for each will be listed and salary ranges will be provided.

The importance of careers in the social sciences must not be minimized. In the world in which we live, we have reached the crossroads between two ages of humankind.

The late CBS foreign correspondent David Schoenbrunn said that we tend to think of the twentieth century as beginning in the year 1900. He, however, regards it as merely a convenient calendar date. The twentieth century, in terms of a break with the past, began with Albert Einstein and his theory of relativity, which he introduced in published form in 1916. Einstein's world was a departure from the earlier world of Isaac Newton, whose theories had dominated scientific thought. In the world of Newton, the basic principle is the law of gravity—that which goes up comes down. In the world of Einstein, there is a totally different gravity—that which goes up high enough stays up and then either circles the earth or goes off into space.

Einstein's discovery ushered in the twentieth century of science and technology. Unfortunately, it did not usher in a twentieth century of the social sciences. In other words, it did not enhance our understanding of what it means to be truly human.

Those who select one of the careers outlined in this book have chosen to correct this situation. They marvel that human beings have traveled to the moon and returned safely to earth. Yet they recognize that, unfortunately, one cannot walk in safety on the streets of many of our cities at night. As long as this inhuman situation exists, there is need for careers in the social sciences. For it is the special mission of social scientists to improve the quality of life for the human race in this and subsequent centuries.

CHAPTER 3

CAREERS IN ANTHROPOLOGY AND SOCIOLOGY

In this chapter, career opportunities in two social sciences, anthropology and sociology, are discussed. These two fields are closely related to each other. Like the other social sciences, they focus on people.

THE SCIENCE OF ANTHROPOLOGY

The term *anthropology* is derived from two Greek words that mean the study of humankind. Anthropologists study people, cultures, and roles in society. They focus on the origins of human life and the physical characteristics of different peoples. Anthropologists investigate the social structures, traditions, customs, and beliefs of people throughout the world.

There are four major specialties in the field of anthropology. Three of them, physical anthropology, archaeology, and linguistics, are related not only to the social sciences but also to the life and behavioral sciences. The fourth field, cultural anthropology, is the one most clearly identified as a social science. It is concerned with peoples and cultures throughout the world.

Cultural anthropologists examine all phases of human life. They study the rites of initiation into a society. They are therefore interested in infant baptism in some Christian religions and the ceremonies associated with birth in African kingdoms that existed even before Christopher Columbus.

Anthropologists also study rites of passage from childhood to adolescence. They are interested in the study of dating, courtship, and marriage rituals.

Cultural anthropologists investigate cultural patterns and behaviors concerning death. They study the burial customs of peoples past and present. For example, when the remains of an early man were found, there were indications that flowers had been buried with him. Cultural anthropologists use evidence like those flowers to learn more about the life and beliefs of people.

The discovery of the tomb of Tutankhamen, king of Egypt from around 1370–1352 B.C., helped cultural anthropologists learn much about life in ancient Egypt. They were able to determine what kinds of foods the ancient Egyptians ate, the games they played, and their favorite leisure activities. They learned about their clothing, homes, occupations, and political institutions. Much of their findings were made after lengthy investigation and detailed observation.

The exciting work of anthropologists continues today. Anthropologists are learning more about the world's people and their cultural heritages.

MAJOR BRANCHES OF ANTHROPOLOGY

Cultural Anthropology

Most anthropologists specialize in cultural anthropology. They study the customs, culture patterns, and social lives of groups. They are as interested in people who live in relative isolation in New Guinea as they are in those who live in modern urban cultures such as New York City. Cultural anthropologists study the similarities and differences between cultures.

Archaeology

Archaeologists study the peoples and cultures from the past. Archaeologists use artifacts and other buried remains to study those who lived before us. They reconstruct past ways of life. They study the groups formed in older societies and their different religious practices. Archaeologists excavate, salvage, and preserve archaeological remains.

A fascinating and newer branch of archaeology is called marine archaeology. Marine archaeologists study sunken ships. Currently, there are several exciting projects being conducted in marine archaeology. These studies are providing us with an understanding of goods traded between nations and life on board ship many years ago.

One of the most interesting marine expeditions lasted nearly twenty years. Margaret Rule, one of the world's leading marine archaeologists, directed the excavation and raising of King Henry VIII's flagship the *Mary Rose*. This ship, named after King Henry's favorite sister, sank on July 19, 1545, as it sailed to fight the Spanish Armada. Centuries later, marine archaeologists found the ship, its contents, and the remains of its crew in the waters of Portsmouth harbor in England. The *Mary Rose* was brought back to Portsmouth in October 1982. There visitors can see King Henry's flagship.

Today's technology is permitting more successful marine expeditions than ever before. Marine archaeologists are learning much about those who lived centuries ago.

Linguistics

Linguistic anthropologists study the role of language in various cultures. They study and describe the dialects, speech patterns, and languages spoken by people throughout the world. Linguistic anthropologists are interested in languages spoken both by people who are living now and by those who lived in the past.

Physical Anthropologists

Physical anthropologists study the evolution of the human body. They look for the first evidences of human life. Physical anthropology is sometimes called biological anthropology. It includes the study of human fossils. Physical anthropologists investigate the lives of primitive beings by studying teeth markings and bone structures.

Fieldwork

Those who work in one of these four branches of anthropology are all concerned with human lives and culture. An important part of each of them is fieldwork. Taking part in an archaeological dig is one example of fieldwork. Another is living in another culture to study the daily lives of the people. A third example of fieldwork is working in a museum of natural history.

CAREERS IN ANTHROPOLOGY

Current Employment Opportunities

Of the approximately ten thousand people in the United States working as anthropologists, it is estimated that 80 percent are employed by colleges and universities. They are responsible for the instruction of undergraduate and graduate students in the four branches of anthropology. Others engage in research projects funded by foundations or granting agencies.

Most of the new jobs in the next few decades will be with government agencies and consulting firms. Openings in the field of anthropology vary greatly and depend on individual talents, education, and professional skills. Recent federal legislation has positively affected employment opportunities in this field. Matching funds for the historical preservation of sites and buildings are now available. There are, then, more career opportunities in this field.

Related Careers

There are many careers related to anthropology. Included are positions in medical research, museums, urban and regional planning, and public health. Service in VISTA and the Peace Corps is also allied to the field of anthropology. Some students study anthropology before entering careers in international business or public administration.

Many students who study anthropology choose careers in museums. Museums are institutions that collect and preserve objects of lasting value. Those who are employed by the museum interpret the meaning or historic, artistic, or scientific significance of the objects housed in the museums.

The objects owned by a museum are called its collection. The word *collection* means that the articles are worth keeping. This, in turn, means that the items in the collection must be cared for and, in some cases, treasured.

Curators Many items in a museum's collection are displayed for people to see. Exhibited or not, all objects in the museum's collections must be registered and stored. Some museum employees, called curators, assign catalog numbers for each group of museum objects.

Artifacts and specimens collected by archaeologists on a field expedition are brought back to the museum where they are registered by the curator.

Once an object is made part of the museum's collection, it must be maintained by the museum's staff. Objects must be kept safe from harm or destruction. Each of them requires very specific methods of preservation.

Conservation Technicians Museums also employ conservation technicians. These employees take care of the items in the collection and restore and repair them. The field of museum conservation has become a highly specialized one.

Education Directors Some museums employ an education director. This is a position that requires both a knowledge of the museum's collection and ways to teach the museum's visitors about it.

Education directors arrange tours and develop audiovisual programs about the collection. They schedule demonstrations and lectures for those visiting the museum.

Salaries and Earnings

Entry-level positions in college teaching in anthropology pay around $34,000 for the academic year. Positions with consulting and government agencies that require a graduate degree in anthropology pay approximately $25,000 for the calendar year.

Positions in social work pay less but usually require only a bachelor's degree. Some positions in anthropology with the federal government have pay ranges from $18,000 to $25,000, depending on the level of education.

Top positions in anthropology offer salaries in excess of $53,000. They are, however, usually reserved for those with a doctorate in anthropology.

Earnings in business and history vary widely, but they are usually about 35 percent higher than in colleges and universities.

PREPARING FOR A CAREER IN ANTHROPOLOGY

High School Preparation

If you are interested in studying anthropology and selecting a career in this field, there are several high school courses that will help you. In addition to mathematics and English composition, classes in biology and history are beneficial. A course in the use of computers is highly recommended because anthropologists today conduct much research using them.

An excellent entry point for someone interested in working as an anthropologist is to work in a museum. Museums frequently have gift shops staffed by volunteers. Some large museums hire students to work in food service areas. Many museums employ interns as docents or guides. Some living museums such as Old Sturbridge Village in Massachusetts and Conner Prairie Pioneer Settlement in Indiana employ interpreters. They play the roles of historical persons and interpret the history of the times for visitors to the museum.

Educational Requirements

Entry-level positions in the field of anthropology require a bachelor's degree. In addition to beginning courses in cultural and physical anthropology and archaeology, courses in psychology, geography, sociology, and physiology are useful.

Graduate work in anthropology is required for all teaching positions at the college and university level.

Most professional anthropologists have postgraduate degrees in their field. Careers in conservation archaeology or medical anthropology require graduate degrees.

SOURCES OF ADDITIONAL INFORMATION

For more information about the field of anthropology, contact:

American Anthropological Association
  4350 North Fairfax Drive
  Suite 640
  Arlington, VA 22203

American Association of Museums
  1225 I Street, NW
  Suite 200
  Washington, DC 20005

Archaeological Institute of America
  656 Beacon Street
  Boston, MA 02215

Association of Science-Technology Centers
  1025 Vermont Avenue, NW
  Suite 500
  Washington, DC 20005

Canadian Sociology and Anthropology Association
  1455, Boulevard de Maisonneuve Ouest
  Montreal, PQ 43G 1M8

Society for American Archaeology
  900 Second Street, NE
  Number 12
  Washington, DC 20002

Society for Applied Anthropology
  P.O. Box 24083
  Oklahoma City, OK 73124

The Smithsonian Institution has published a directory of museum training programs and internships offered by universities and museums. It is available for six dollars from the Smithsonian's Office of Museum Programs. Its address is P.O. Box 274 81-OMP, Washington, DC 20013.

THE SCIENCE OF SOCIOLOGY

Sociology is the study of how people relate to each other in their homes, at work, and in all other facets of life. It focuses, too, on how the group affects the individual.

Sociologists rely on the scientific method as the principal tool in explaining and predicting human relations. In using the scientific method, sociologists recognize a problem and, through observation and experimentation, collect data that enable them to form and test hypotheses. They work with people and study their ways of acting and interacting and their response to the world around them.

Sociologists Study Groups

Sociologists analyze the behavior of groups or social systems such as families and neighborhoods. Because sociology is the study of people in a social context, sociologists generally do not study individuals. Indeed, the term *sociology* comes from two Latin and Greek words that mean the study of groups. Sociologists focus on two areas: 1) the social relationships of those who belong to the group, and 2) the beliefs and values that are held by those in the group. In other words, sociologists study human society by examining the groups that people form.

Groups are made up of individuals who have something in common. An example used by sociologists to show what is meant by a group involves people on an elevator. When they get on the elevator, they each have their own plans and purposes. When the elevator malfunctions, they join together and plan their exit. This collection of individuals becomes a group with a common goal.

Humans form groups for many purposes. Each of these groups is a focus of study by sociologists.

Religious Groups Frequently, people study nature and life about them and conclude that there is some superior being that is responsible for what they see. They identify this superior being as God, Allah, Yahweh, Buddha, or some other name and then join together to worship him. A religion or way of life is then founded. These groups are studied in courses in the sociology of religion.

Educational Systems A second example of a group is the American educational system. Historically, young children were taught at home. When the knowledge to be taught became more complex, societies formed schools to educate their children. Sociologists study the educational systems throughout the world. They investigate the role of parents in education and the training of teachers. They examine the forces that determine the subjects taught in schools throughout the world. Today there are sociologists who specialize in the sociology of education.

Families A final example of groups studied by sociologists is the family. The structure of families is not the same in all human societies.

Many Chinese Americans have extended families. An extended family is one that includes several generations in one household. In some extended families, all important decisions are made by the oldest man in the family.

Some families are ruled by the oldest woman. Sociologists call them matriarchal families. Several native American tribes were matriarchal societies.

Thirty years ago, the most common white, middle-class family pattern in the United States was the nuclear family. Nuclear families are made up of a man and woman who are married to each other and live with their children. In the past several decades, this pattern has changed. Today, many white, middle-class families are made up of single parents who live with their children.

Some families' structures have been changed by death, separation, or divorce. Sociologists study the roles and interactions in these families, which they call fractured or broken.

In the last several years, a different family structure has become very common. Frequently one parent in a fractured family marries another. They and their children become a

new family. Sociologists call this type of family structure a blended family.

Some families in the United States are called matrifocal families by sociologists. *Matrifocal* means that the focus of the family is on the mother or oldest woman. Today many single mothers must work, and they rely on others to help care for their children.

Sociologists Study Change

Sociologists know that society changes. They study the effects of these changes in all facets of life.

For example, sociologists study the graying of America. This phrase describes the growing number of older people in our society. The study of the social and personal problems faced by those growing older is the focus of sociologists who specialize in gerontology.

There are many other areas of study investigated by sociologists. They are, simply, interested in all groups formed by people in our society.

Some of the areas in which sociologists specialize are:

- Social organization—the study of the makeup and purpose of social groups.
- Urban sociology—the study of conditions in cities such as crime rates and housing patterns.
- Criminology—the study of crime, crime prevention, and punishment.

- Gerontology—the study of aging and the special personal and social problems of older people.
- Demography—the study of the size, characteristics, and movement of population.

CAREERS IN SOCIOLOGY

In 1996 sociologists held several thousand jobs. Many sociologists are employed by government agencies. They deal with urban crime, poverty, public assistance programs, and racial relations. Sociologists in these areas are hired by the federal government to work in the Department of Health and Human Services.

Sociologists specializing in demography work for the Bureau of the Census and international organizations such as the United Nations and the World Health Organization.

State and local governments employ sociologists who specialize in criminology. They work primarily for law enforcement agencies.

Some sociologists are self-employed. They have private practices in counseling or research. They are often employed by the areas of business, industry, and education as consultants.

Sociologists who study the social factors that affect mental and public health are employed by hospitals and welfare organizations.

Other sociologists are involved in research. They collect information and analyze data. They also evaluate different kinds of social programs. Very often they use statistical techniques and computers in their work.

Some sociologists are administrators. They manage social service programs and child welfare agencies.

In addition to these many different jobs, about thirteen thousand sociologists teach in American colleges and universities. There they teach undergraduate and graduate students enrolled in sociology courses.

Related Careers

Several career choices in fields allied to sociology are possible. Included are occupations in social policy and planning. The following careers are some of those in which an understanding of sociology is valuable.

Law Enforcement Many police officers and law enforcement personnel have taken courses in sociology. Their responsibilities include directing traffic and investigating crimes.

Law enforcement officers are involved in community affairs. Frequently, they meet with groups of citizens and try to increase their confidence in the police. Law enforcement officers also teach community groups how to help fight crime.

Human Service Workers Today there are many paraprofessional jobs in human services agencies. They involve working in group homes and halfway houses. Human service workers also are employed by community mental health centers and substance abuse programs. Some are community outreach workers and others are social work assistants.

All human services workers are under the direction of professional staff members. Job duties of human services workers vary, depending on the people receiving services.

Human services workers in health care settings lead groups, organize activities, and counsel clients. Some of them handle administrative jobs.

Others who work in social service agencies help clients. They interview their clients and determine how the agency can help them. Many human services workers maintain records and files. Case aides assist clients in many ways. They accompany them to adult day-care programs or doctors' offices.

Some work in public housing projects. They help the tenants by providing information about regulations and services.

Human services workers are employed in group homes. There they help adults who need some supervision or assistance on a daily basis.

Recreation Workers Recreation workers plan activities that help others enjoy their leisure time. They are employed by health clubs, theme parks, campgrounds, and senior centers.

Others are hired by adult day-care programs, nursing homes, and correctional institutions. Many recreation workers are employed by organizations such as the Girl Scouts and Red Cross.

A large number of recreation workers are part-time employees. Some part-time, seasonal jobs include playground leaders and camp counselors.

Employment Opportunities

Of the nineteen thousand people working as sociologists, 80 percent of them are employed by colleges and universities. The U.S. Department of Labor predicts strong competition for people seeking positions at any level.

Sociologists trained in research methods, advanced statistics, and the use of computers will have the widest choice of jobs. Demand is expected to be strong for research personnel in the areas of rural sociology, community development, population analysis, public opinion research, medical sociology, juvenile delinquency, and evaluation research.

Students who major in gerontology are expected to find a growing number of career opportunities through the next decade. In addition to gerontology, other areas of demand will be demography and criminology.

Sociologists will also be needed to administer and evaluate programs intended to cope with social and welfare problems.

It is expected that the number of those graduating with advanced degrees in sociology will be greater than the number of available jobs.

Those with doctorates in sociology will face keen competition for faculty positions. An increasing number of those with Ph.D.s in sociology will be employed by government agencies and research organizations. Those skilled in research methods, including survey techniques, statistics, and computer science, will have the most job opportunities.

Those with master's degrees will face much competition for positions in research firms, business, and government. They will find very few academic positions, even in junior colleges.

Graduates with bachelor's degrees in sociology will find some entry-level positions in business, industry, and government.

Salaries and Earnings

Sociologists employed by educational institutions earn an average of about $44,500 a year. Those in business and industry earn about $57,000.

In 1996, the average entry-level salary for sociologists with a bachelor's degree ranged from $18,500 to $24,000. The starting salary for those with a master's degree was about $31,000 a year.

Sociologists with a Ph.D. earn about $34,000 in entry-level positions. In general, sociologists with a doctoral degree earn significantly more than those who have not received one.

PREPARING FOR A CAREER IN SOCIOLOGY

High School Preparation

To prepare to study sociology at a college or university, you should take high school courses in academic English, mathematics, and the social, biological, and physical sciences. You will also find it helpful to learn as much as possible about computers.

Working with people in groups is also an excellent preparation. For example, if you are interested in a career in gerontology, you might work as a volunteer in a nursing home or senior citizen center.

Other job opportunities that will help you are assisting in playground activities or youth programs.

Educational Requirements

A bachelor's degree is essential for any entry-level position, and a master's degree is recommended, or in many instances, required. A Ph.D. is necessary for positions in most colleges and universities. The doctorate is also required for research project directors, administrative positions, or consultants. It is expected that as the job market tightens through the next decade, a Ph.D. will be required for all professional and academic positions in sociology.

Sociologists with master's degrees are employed in administrative and research positions by private industries and public agencies. Some may obtain teaching positions in junior colleges.

Those who have earned a bachelor's degree in sociology find jobs in related fields. Some work as counselors or recreation directors in public and private agencies.

Others who hold a bachelor's degree are hired as interviewers by social service agencies.

Those who meet state requirements for teacher certification may become sociology teachers in secondary schools.

A degree in sociology provides an excellent preparation for those planning careers in law, journalism, and social work.

For many paraprofessional positions, an associate degree in sociology is desired. Included are such career options as recreation workers and human services workers.

SOURCES OF ADDITIONAL INFORMATION

For more information about careers in sociology, contact:

American Society of Criminology
   1314 Kinnear Road
   Suite 212
   Columbus, OH 43212

American Sociological Association
   1771 N Street, NW
   Washington, DC 20036

Canadian Sociology and Anthropology Association
   1455, Boulevard de Maisonneuve Ouest
   Montreal, PQ 43G 1M8

Gerontology Society
   1835 K Street, NW
   Washington, DC 20006

Population Association of America
   806 Fifteenth Street, NW
   Suite 640
   Washington, DC 20005

Population Reference Bureau
   1337 Connecticut Avenue, NW
   Washington, DC 20036

Sociological Practice Association
   RD 2, Box 141 A
   Chester, NY 10918

Additional information about careers in selected allied fields is available from:

American Association for Leisure and Recreation
  3101 Park Center Drive
  Alexandria, VA 22302

American Camping Association
  Bradford Woods
  5000 State Road 67 N
  Martinsville, IN 46151

Canadian Association of Schools of Social Work
  100-B, 30 Rosemount Avenue
  Ottawa, ON K1Y 154

Council on Standards in Human Service Education
  Montgomery Community College
  Blue Bell, PA 19422

National Employee Services and Recreation Association
  2400 South Downing Street
  Westchester, IL 60153

National Organization for Human Service Education
  2840 Sheridan Road
  Evanston, IL 60201

Social Science Federation of Canada
  #415, 151 Slater Street
  Ottawa, ON K1P 5H3

The American Sociological Association has many publications that will help those desiring more information about opportunities in sociology. Among them are:

- *Careers in Sociology.* Single copies of this excellent booklet are available without charge from the executive office of the American Sociological Association (ASA). Multiple copies are twenty-five cents each.
- *Majoring in Sociology: A Guide for Students.* Single copies of this publication, designed for high school and undergraduate students, are available free from the ASA executive office. Multiple copies are five cents each.
- *Career Possibilities for Sociology Graduates.* Single copies of this publication for those who have degrees in sociology are available without charge from ASA. Multiple copies are fifteen cents each.

CHAPTER 4

CAREERS IN PSYCHOLOGY

Have you ever wondered why people behave or act as they do? Psychology is the social science that studies the human mind and human behavior. Indeed, the word psychology is derived from two Greek words that mean the study of the mind.

The term *mind* means much more than the word *brain.* The mind is that part of human beings that thinks, feels, chooses, decides, and perceives. Thus, psychology, the study of the mind, focuses on thinking processes, feelings, and behavior.

Psychologists investigate a person's ability to think and the effect of emotions on human health and behavior. Psychologists use their skills and training to counsel or advise individuals and groups.

Psychologists make up the largest occupation in the social sciences. More than 130,000 people work in the field of psychology. Most of them are employed in the areas of research and counseling.

Yet psychology is a relatively new science. It did not even exist at the time of the American Revolution. Only within the past forty-five years has psychology become a career field.

If you choose a career in psychology, you will have to study for many years. A bachelor's degree with a major in psychology is usually not enough for you to qualify for a job in the field. The best positions in psychology require a doctoral degree.

MAJOR BRANCHES OF PSYCHOLOGY

Experimental Psychologists

Experimental psychologists make up the largest group in psychological research. They study human beings and sometimes study animals such as mice, rats, and monkeys. Experimental psychologists are researchers who try to better understand human behavior.

They design and conduct research in laboratories on college campuses and in large industries. Some experimental psychologists are involved in research for the government.

Experimental psychologists use observation and measurement techniques. Because they conduct many experiments, they must know statistics. Advanced courses in probability, which is used to predict results, and inferential statistics are required as part of the training of experimental psychologists. Because experimental psychologists process much information, they use computers in their work.

Though they may work in private industry or in laboratories, most experimental psychologists teach in colleges and universities.

A Ph.D. is required for careers in the field of experimental psychology.

Industrial Psychologists

Industrial psychologists are concerned with human behavior in the workplace. They are concerned with such aspects of work as job satisfaction, efficiency, and employee training programs. Industrial psychology is concerned with the individual employees in an organization. People working in this field investigate working conditions and the relationships that exist between employers and employees. Industrial psychologists develop plans for changing an organization's structure to improve its productivity and to increase employee satisfaction.

Simply, industrial psychologists are involved in the world of work. They examine the work environment and identify those things that will increase productivity and employee satisfaction. They apply psychological techniques to personnel administration, management, and marketing. They screen job applicants and take part in employee training and development.

Industrial psychologists generally hold doctorates in their field of study. They are employed in business, industry, and government facilities.

Clinical Psychologists

Clinical psychologists are interested in working with people who have emotional problems. They look for causes of emotional or attitudinal problems in their clients. They then diagnose and treat them. Clinical psychologists help the mentally or emotionally ill adjust to life. They work directly with their patients to find out the causes of their problems. Psychological testing is a major part of their work.

The greatest number of employment opportunities exists for clinical psychologists who have doctoral degrees. Clinical psychologists must usually complete an internship during their training. All states require that clinical psychologists pass licensing exams. In order to take the licensing examination, the candidate must have a doctorate in clinical psychology.

Some clinical psychologists are employed by hospitals and clinics. Others have private practices where they treat clients.

Clinical psychologists sometimes work with physicians and other professionals in developing treatment programs. They may also administer community or state mental health programs.

Some clinical psychologists teach at the university level. There they train graduate students who are preparing for careers in clinical psychology.

Developmental Psychologists

Developmental psychologists trace the stages of human growth from birth to death. They study the patterns and causes of changes in people's behavior as they pass through life. Developmental psychologists realize that people think, see, and behave differently during their lifetimes.

Some developmental psychologists specialize in human behavior during infancy, childhood, and adolescence. Others study the many changes that take place as people mature and age.

Developmental psychologists study human nature. They know the sequences of normal human development and the problems that result when this development is not normal.

Educational Psychologists

Educational psychologists study the learning process. They investigate intellectual growth. Educational psychologists use their knowledge of child development to help teachers plan courses and school activities that are appropriate for the pupils' level of development.

Educational psychologists analyze the educational needs of their clients. They frequently develop instructional materials and assess their effectiveness.

Educational psychologists are employed in education, business, and industry. Some are hired by the armed services to evaluate their instructional programs. Many teach students in colleges and universities.

A Ph.D. is usually required for positions in educational psychology.

Social Psychologists

Social psychologists study how individuals perceive or regard each other. They frequently work with groups, studying group behaviors and attitudes.

They examine people's interactions with others. They focus on the social environment in which they live. Some of the areas of specialization for social psychologists are group behavior, leadership, and group attitudes.

Social psychology is often a research specialty. Social psychologists engaged in research are concerned with the behavior of people in groups.

Counseling Psychologists

Counseling psychologists help people with the daily problems of life. Each year, about thirty-four million Americans seek the help of counseling psychologists. Counseling psychology, not surprisingly, is the area in the field that is most familiar to many Americans.

Counseling psychologists are trained in testing procedures. They interview and counsel clients. Typically, counseling psychologists work with normal or moderately maladjusted persons in hospitals, mental health centers, or facilities in rehabilitation.

They use many techniques to advise people on how to deal with problems of everyday life. Counseling psychologists are concerned with their clients' personal, social, educational, and vocational lives.

There are several fields of specialization in counseling psychology.

Rehabilitation Counselors help those with disabilities become more self-sufficient. They evaluate their clients' individual potential for employment.

Many rehabilitation counselors work in health facilities, Department of Veterans Affairs hospitals, and substance abuse clinics.

Employment Counselors help individuals make wise career decisions. They help their clients explore and evaluate their education, training, and skills. They may arrange for them to take aptitude and achievement tests. They also help clients find jobs and complete the application forms needed in new positions.

Employment counselors are employed by nonprofit organizations such as Goodwill and by social agencies such as community centers. Some are employed by colleges and vocational schools where they help the students find employment.

Mental Health Counselors help individuals and families deal with family conflicts, substance abuse, and problems at work. Some mental health counselors help rape victims. Many counsel families coping with illness and death. Mental health counselors cooperate with other professionals, such as psychiatrists, social workers, and psychologists.

A master's degree is generally required for counselors.

School Psychologists

School psychologists work in elementary and secondary schools. They help pupils individually and in groups with their concerns, plans, goals, and achievement. They test pupils who seem to have learning problems.

School psychologists develop individualized programs for pupils with learning disabilities. They work closely with teachers and consult with them about the developmental needs of individual students. They work with pupils, their parents, and teachers to resolve behavior problems.

Some school psychologists are also psychometrists. They administer and interpret standardized examinations such as intelligence tests and personality surveys.

Counselors in secondary schools establish career information centers and run career education programs. They advise the students on college admission requirements, entrance exams, and financial aid. They provide information on trade and technical schools and apprenticeship programs.

Frequently, high school counselors help students find part-time and seasonal employment. They help students understand and cope with their social and personal problems. High school counselors increasingly are responsible for running drug and alcohol abuse programs.

Most elementary and secondary school counselors work the traditional school year. However, an increasing number of school districts are employing school counselors on eleven-month contracts.

School psychology is closely related to the fields of educational and developmental psychology. It is a graduate specialty in many master's degree programs.

RELATED CAREERS

There are many career opportunities in fields related to psychology. Indeed, courses in psychology are valuable for those who select careers in teaching, social work, and religion.

Protestant ministers, Catholic priests, and Jewish rabbis spend much time counseling those who are members of their faith. They advise individuals seeking guidance, visit the sick, and console the bereaved. Because they frequently work with groups, training in social psychology is extremely beneficial.

EMPLOYMENT OPPORTUNITIES

The prospects for teachers and researchers in the field of psychology in four-year colleges or universities are presently limited. Some two-year colleges are adding faculty.

Positions in psychological research depend on funding to support research programs. Federal and state funding are not expected to increase significantly. Some private foundations support research programs to investigate human behavior.

The current growth in regional and local mental health facilities will open more employment opportunities.

The increase in services provided for senior citizens indicates a need for more professionals trained in psychology to work with older people.

Employment opportunities are excellent in fields such as counseling psychology, industrial psychology, and clinical psychology.

SALARIES AND EARNINGS

Salaries for beginning college and university instructors in psychology range from $26,000 to $34,000. Psychologists in private practice typically have the highest incomes. They usually earn over $55,000.

Considering the years of study needed to obtain a doctorate in psychology, salaries for those not in private practice are not high. The average income for a person who has a doctorate in psychology is about $45,000 a year.

The salaries for psychologists who teach in colleges and universities range from $26,000 to $57,000 a year. Many psychologists earn additional money through consulting or as members of a group practice.

PREPARING FOR A CAREER IN PSYCHOLOGY

High School Preparation

Probably the most important high school preparation for a major in psychology is a firm foundation in mathematics and English composition. A knowledge of computers is essential in the field of psychology. If you can, take a course in computers and their use while in high school.

If you are interested in a career in psychology and if your high school offers a course in psychology, you would be wise to take it. It will introduce you to many of the topics you will study if you major or minor in psychology at a college or university.

Educational Requirements

All of the professional positions in psychology require a minimum of a bachelor's degree in psychology from a college or university. Most professional positions in the field require additional study beyond the undergraduate degree. Many require a doctorate.

Some state or community agencies, however, offer a limited number of positions for graduates with bachelor's degrees in psychology. In addition, many psychology majors obtain positions in business and industry.

Recently there has been an increase in the paraprofessional career opportunities in some fields of psychology such as mental health assistant. Mental health assistants are paraprofessionals in a facility such as a mental health center or senior citizen service center. A mental health assistant's duties include screening and evaluating new clients, contacting patients, and keeping records. For this position, an associate degree in psychology is usually sufficient, although a bachelor's degree is preferred.

SOURCES OF ADDITIONAL INFORMATION

For more information about careers in psychology, contact:

American Association for Counseling and Development
5999 Stevenson Avenue
Alexandria, VA 22304

American Association of State Psychology Boards
P.O. Box 4389
Montgomery, AL 36103

American Psychiatric Association
  1400 K Street, NW
  Washington, DC 20005

American Psychological Association
  Educational Affairs Office
  1200 Seventeenth Street, NW
  Washington, DC 20036

American School Counselor Association
  5999 Stevenson Avenue
  Alexandria, VA 22304

Canadian Psychological Association
  #20, 151 Slater Street
  Ottawa, ON K1P 5H3

Commission on Rehabilitation Counselor Certification
  1156 Shure Drive, Suite 350
  Arlington Heights, IL 60004

Council for Accreditation of Counseling and Related
    Educational Programs
  American Association for Counseling and Development
  5999 Stevenson Avenue
  Alexandria, VA 22304

Council on Rehabilitation Education
  185 North Wabash Street
  Room 1617
  Chicago, IL 60601

Division of Resource Development
  Rehabilitation Services Administration
  U.S. Department of Education
  330 C Street, SW
  Washington, DC 20202

National Academy of Certified Clinical Mental Health
    Counselors
  5999 Stevenson Avenue
  Alexandria, VA 22304

National Association of School Psychology
  1511 K Street, NW
  Suite 716
  Washington, DC 20005

National Board for Certified Counselors
  5999 Stevenson Avenue
  Alexandria, VA 22304

National Council on Rehabilitation Education
  c/o Maddux O'Malley, Inc.
  2921 Ermine Way
  Farmers Branch, TX 75234

National Mental Health Association
  1021 Prince Street
  Arlington, VA 22314

National Rehabilitation Counseling Association
  633 South Washington Street
  Alexandria, VA 22314

For more information about careers as religious workers, contact:

Beth Medrash Govoha Seminary
   626 Seventh Street
   Lakewood, NJ 08701
   (Orthodox)

Hebrew Union College
   Jewish Institute of Religion
   Director of Admissions
   One Fourth Street
   New York, NY 10012
   (Reform)

The Jewish Theological Seminary of America
   3080 Broadway
   New York, NY 10027
   (Conservative)

National Conference of Diocesan Vocation Directors
   1307 South Wabash Avenue
   Chicago, IL 60605

National Council of Churches
   Professional Church Leadership
   Room 770
   475 Riverside Drive
   New York, NY 10115

The Rabbi Isaac Elchanan Theological Seminary
  2540 Amsterdam Avenue
  New York, NY 10033
  (Orthodox)

Reconstructionist Rabbinical College
  Church Road and Greenwood Avenue
  Wyncote, PA 19095

Serra International
  22 West Monroe Street
  Chicago, IL 60603

CHAPTER 5

CAREERS IN HISTORY AND GEOGRAPHY

History and geography are the oldest social sciences. They were studied by those who lived in ancient times. They are studied today to help us plan for the future.

HISTORY

If you want to understand why events happen the way they do or if you would like to know about people's values, you have a good reason to study history. If you enjoy stories about the choices people make and the events that result from their choices or if you like to solve mysteries about people, places, and events, you should consider studying history.

At a time when businesses and universities demand more and more specialized knowledge, the study of history still sheds light on how past events affect the present and future. Learning about the past can give you insight into the motivating forces of human life: love and hate, oppression and reform, hope and despair, wealth and poverty. The study of history can prepare you for everyday life by helping you understand how people have tried to solve their problems. As twentieth-century French writer and art historian André Malraux observed, "Our heritage is composed of all the voices that can answer our questions."

Divisions of History

Because history is concerned about the past of the world's peoples, its scope is tremendous. There is so much to study in history that its subject matter is divided in several ways.

TIME

Its first division is based on time, or when the people being studied lived. Historians divide historic events into three periods: ancient, medieval, and modern.

Ancient history includes the time when records of the past were first kept through the earliest centuries after the birth of Christ. Some of the people studied in ancient history are the Greeks, Romans, Chinese, and Egyptians.

The second time period is the medieval, or Middle Ages. It includes the events that took place several centuries after the birth of Christ through those that occurred in the seventeenth century. Some of the peoples studied during this period are the Crusaders, explorers such as Christopher

Columbus and Marco Polo, and Henry VIII, king of England.

Modern times is the third division. Included in a study of modern history are the peoples who lived from about 1700 to the present. Some of the events that took place during this period are the founding of the American nation and World War II.

GEOGRAPHY

The subject matter of history can also be divided by geography. In other words, the content is studied by nation or region. Included in this division are American history, western civilization, world history, and nonwestern studies.

TOPICS

Finally, the subject matter of history can be divided by topics. Included in this division are the American Civil War, the Industrial Revolution, and the Age of Enlightenment, for example.

No matter how it is divided, history is a fascinating study. Sometimes students complain that it is boring and simply the memorization of names and dates. It is unfortunate that this probably is true because of the way it is presented. In reality, history should be a fascinating study. It is, after all, concerned with our past. Its study will help us face the future. History then should not be presented as a listing of people, places, dates, and events. It should be presented as an area of study that helps us use our judgment in truly human ways.

Areas of Specialization

There are four major areas of specialization in history.

Social history examines the people in history. Some topics included in social history are immigration, industrialization, and urbanization.

Economic history investigates how people through the ages have provided for their wants and needs. Some topics included in economic history are the plantation system and labor organizations.

Political history is the study of how people through the ages have been governed. Included in a study of political history are the wars resulting from revolutions and Nazi Germany.

Cultural history focuses on the values, beliefs, goals, and lifestyles of people who lived before us. Cultural history includes a review of a people's art, music, literature, and philosophy. Included in a study of cultural history are topics such as Marxist communism and the Catholic Church in the Middle Ages.

If you love the study of history, you may decide to continue your studies. You may decide to select one of the career opportunities in history.

MAJOR CAREERS IN HISTORY

Professional Historians

Professional historians describe and analyze the events of the past through writing and research. They relate knowledge of the past to the present. Historians specialize in one or more branches of history.

They focus on national or regional history; ancient, medieval, or modern periods; or in the history of a field such as economics, politics, war, religion, music, or architecture. Other fields they might choose include oral history, popular culture, genealogy, and ethnic history.

Oral history involves speaking with those who have lived during a specific time and recording conversations with them. Interviewing a soldier who fought in Vietnam is an example of oral history.

Popular culture is concerned with people's values, activities, and preferences. Analyzing how John Wayne's films shaped modern culture's perceptions of the Old West is an example of an activity in which a historian who specializes in popular culture might be involved.

Genealogy is the study of family histories. Many historians focus on genealogical studies.

Ethnic history is another specialty of some historians. Investigating the influence of Americans of Bohemian descent in Cleveland, Ohio, is an example of ethnic studies.

Professional historians prepare in narrative or outline form a chronological record of past and current events dealing with a specific phase of human activity. They gather historical data from indexes, catalogs, archives, court records, news files, diaries, and other published and unpublished materials. Professional historians judge these data on the basis of authenticity and their meaning. They also can engage in historical research for individuals, institutions, and organizations.

Archivists

Archivists evaluate and edit permanent records and historical documents. They are not only involved in research based on materials in archives, but they also direct the safekeeping of archival documents. They frequently must establish the date of a document's origin to determine its historical value. They often prepare document descriptions and reference materials.

Archivists decide what parts of the information produced by the government, schools and colleges, corporations, and other organizations should be made part of a historical record. Frequently, they decide which items of their archival collection should be exhibited. Their collections may include coins, stamps, photographs, documents, clothing, maps, buildings, and historic sites.

Archivists also classify the information in their collections so it can be easily located. They decide whether it should be stored in its original form or if it should be stored on microfilm or as computer records.

Archivists are employed by museums or special corporate, medical, or private libraries and historical societies. There they assemble, analyze, preserve, and index documentary material for scholarly use.

Historical Consultants

Historical consultants assist editors, publishers, filmmakers, and television producers of historically oriented materials. When you next view a historical film or documentary, read the credits. Frequently you will find the name of a historian who helped in its production.

Teachers

Many historians are employed by colleges and universities. There they teach undergraduate students enrolled in history survey classes, and they also teach in their area of specialization. They instruct graduate students and advise them as they complete their advanced studies.

RELATED CAREERS

History majors often enter law schools or business professional schools. They are also employed in fields including business, labor, industry, communication, and government civil service.

Students who combine history with strong backgrounds in other subjects may work in such careers as journalism and public service. Businesses are interested in hiring people with the broad educational background that history majors have.

Persons with historical training are especially well suited for work in government careers. History students have a real advantage when taking the various civil service examinations. History graduates can find jobs in diplomatic and welfare services and governmental research and record keeping at the local, state, and national levels.

For employment in fields allied to history, training in a foreign language is desirable. In some, such as the foreign service, it is mandatory.

EMPLOYMENT OPPORTUNITIES

Opportunities for employment rest largely with an individual's training and determination. The employment potential in the field of history is limited through the next decade.

The best prospects for archivists are with government agencies. There are, however, few openings in museums. Some archivists are employed by large corporations.

SALARIES AND EARNINGS

The national average starting salary for professional historians is $33,000. Archivists generally earn an average of $28,000 the first year of employment.

The average starting salary for historians employed by government and nonprofit organizations is $22,000.

Most professional historians supplement their regular salaries by consulting, lecturing, and writing.

EDUCATIONAL REQUIREMENTS

Advanced education and the acquisition of research skills are key factors in promotion in the field of history.

A Ph.D. is a minimum requirement for history faculty in four-year colleges and universities. Positions as archivists usually require a master's degree or Ph.D.

SOURCES OF ADDITIONAL INFORMATION

For more information about careers in history, contact:

American Association for State and Local History
   172 Second Avenue N
   Suite 102
   Nashville, TN 37210

American Historical Association
  400 A Street, SE
  Washington, DC 20003

American Institute for Conservation of Historic
    and Artistic Works
  3545 Williamsburg Lane, NW
  Washington, DC 20008

Canadian Council of Archives
  West Memorial Bldg., #1109
  344 Wellington Street
  Ottawa, ON K1A ON3

Canadian Historical Association
  395 Wellington Street
  Ottawa, ON K1A ON3

National Center for the Study of History, Inc.
  Drawer 730
  Germantown, MD 20874

National Trust for Historic Preservation
  1785 Massachusetts Avenue, NW
  Washington, DC 20036

Office of Museum Programs
  The Smithsonian Institution
  Arts and Industries Building, Room 2235
  Washington, DC 20560

Organization of American Historians
  112 North Bryan Street
  Bloomington, IN 47401

Society of American Archivists
  600 South Federal Street, Suite 504
  Chicago, IL 60605

GEOGRAPHY

Geographers focus on the relationship between people and their environment and their dependency upon each other. They describe the problems that arise in this type of relationship.

The word *geography* is derived from two Greek words, one which means writings or drawings, and the other meaning earth. This term is an apt one for a science that studies impressions such as mountains, hills, and valleys. But geography is a social science. This means that geographers study the various interrelationships of humans and their environment.

Geography is not just the study of where, how long, how far, and how high. It is the study of the earth's surface and the way that different environments affect the people who live there. It is also the way people affect the places where they live.

Generally, geography is divided into two areas: physical geography and human geography.

Usually physical geography is not regarded as a social science. Most people regard physical geography as one of the physical sciences.

Human geography, which includes such areas as cultural geography, urban geography, ecological geography, and political geography, is regarded as a social science. In each of these areas of study, humans are an important part of the geographer's work.

Like history, geography is often disliked by students in elementary and secondary schools. But when the truly social aspect of these disciplines is introduced, they cannot be uninspiring or boring.

For example, human geography can explain why high school basketball is such a phenomenon in the state of Indiana. So enthused are its fans during the tournaments that lead to the state championship that the period is described as Hoosier hysteria. The reasons for Indiana's fascination with high school basketball lie in the state's history, economics, and, particularly, its geography.

About one hundred years ago, Indiana was primarily an agricultural state. This means that most people who lived there earned their living by farming. Farmers led very busy lives and worked very long hours. Their busiest seasons were spring, when they planted their crops; summer, when they tended them; and fall, when they harvested them. During the winter, because of the cold and snow, farmers had fewer responsibilities. They cared for their animals and kept their equipment in good repair.

During the winter months, the children who lived and worked on the family farms had more leisure time, just as their parents did. They attended small, nearby schools that did not have much money for recreational equipment.

Each of these factors is important. Basketball requires far fewer players than sports such as football. It requires little equipment other than a ball and hoop. A player's shooting skills can be developed by practice with no other players involved.

All of these factors combined caused basketball to have a firm hold on Indiana's people. The tradition of a century continues today, so that Indiana's enthusiasm for the sport is known around the world.

One other example of the human side of geography is seen in the names of professional sports teams. The Milwaukee Brewers, Green Bay Packers, and Detroit Pistons all have names that have their roots in the work many people did in the cities where they are located.

This human approach to geography can make study in the field fascinating. Perhaps more importantly, knowledge of geography will help the people of today take care of the world around them.

MAJOR CAREERS IN GEOGRAPHY

Cartographers

Cartographers make maps. Some of the maps they make include physical maps that show continents, oceans, and features such as mountains and rivers. Political maps show boundaries of states, provinces, and countries. Another kind of map is a population density map, which shows how many people live in a specific area.

Others who are involved in cartography are organizers, researchers, managers, and photographers. Cartographers are frequently employed by the government and in industry.

Urban and Regional Planners

Urban and regional planners develop plans for the orderly growth of communities. They must have training in geography in addition to planning. They are concerned with land use for residential, business, and community purposes. They suggest ways to use land more efficiently. They study the types of industries in a community, characteristics of the people who live there, and employment and economic trends.

Urban and regional planners are concerned with such things as the location of schools, streets and highways, water lines, and recreational sites. In large organizations, urban and regional planners specialize in areas such as physical design, public transportation, and community relations. Many urban and regional planners are concerned with the renovation of rundown business districts. They are also concerned with the reconstruction and preservation of historic buildings.

Some urban and regional planners are employed by departments of planning of cities and states. Others are employed by community development agencies. Some urban and regional planners are hired by architectural and surveying firms and large land developers.

In 1996, urban and regional planners held about twenty-two thousand jobs. According to the Department of Labor, local government planning agencies such as cities and counties employed over 66 percent of them.

Teachers

Some geographers teach undergraduates who are studying geography in universities and colleges. Others train graduate students for careers as professional geographers and researchers.

Geographers in Government

Geographers in government and industry are usually not called by that name. They frequently have such titles as intelligence officer, transportation coordinator, political analyst, and planning director. The Central Intelligence Agency and Defense Mapping Agency employ most of the geographers in the federal government.

RELATED CAREERS

Many careers are allied with the field of geography. Some of the job titles are map curator, aerial photo interpreter, real estate consultant, meteorologist, and travel agent.

Travel agents have become increasingly important since airline deregulation. More and more air carriers are passing the responsibility of reservations and ticketing to them. For this reason, it is expected that there will be very strong growth in the travel industry through the next decade.

Travel agents help consumers book flights, hotel rooms, and car rentals. They have traditionally served business travelers, but with more people traveling for leisure, their workload has increased significantly.

Travel agents' salaries vary greatly. Earnings are generally based on commissions paid by the airlines, hotels, tour companies, and car rental agencies.

EMPLOYMENT OPPORTUNITIES

About 25 percent of all professional geographers find employment in local, state, or federal government; the armed services; or international organizations.

The greatest demand for geographers is in geographic information systems and other areas of technical data interpretation, remote sensing and cartography, planning, market research, and site analysis.

Employment for planning professionals is expected to grow more slowly than the average for all occupations through the mid-1990s. People who specialize have better opportunities, and much new growth is occurring in private consulting firms rather than with government agencies.

SALARIES AND EARNINGS

Salaries are variable depending upon education levels, skills, place of employment, and demand. For a beginning geographer with a bachelor's degree, salaries range from $18,000 to $24,000. An experienced cartographer employed by the federal government can earn over $40,000 annually.

A beginning instructor of geography at a four-year college earns about $35,000 for the academic year.

State agencies pay urban and regional planners more than city, county, or regional governments. The average annual salary paid by the state was $37,000. That paid by the local governments was $34,000. Salaries of planners in large areas may be as much as $10,000 a year higher than those of planners in smaller ones.

Salaries of urban and regional planners employed by the federal government averaged $44,500 annually in 1996.

PREPARING FOR A CAREER IN GEOGRAPHY

High School Preparation

If you are preparing for a career in geography, several courses in high school will help you. A solid foundation in communication skills is essential. If your high school offers courses in world or human geography, it would be beneficial to take them. A course in computer science would be extremely advantageous.

Educational Requirements

An undergraduate degree in geography is necessary for most entry-level positions in geography. However, a four-year degree may not be essential for some entry-level positions in the field of cartography.

Four-year colleges and universities require a doctoral degree for positions in teaching and research. A master's degree is required for teaching in two-year colleges and technical schools.

SOURCES OF ADDITIONAL INFORMATION

For more information about careers in the field of geography, contact:

American Congress on Surveying and Mapping
  210 Little Falls Street
  Falls Church, VA 22046

Association of American Geographers
  1710 Sixteenth Street, NW
  Washington, DC 20009

Canadian Association of Geographers
  Burnside Hall, McGill University
  805 Rue Sherbrooke Ouest
  Montreal, PQ H3A 2K6

Additional information on careers in urban and regional planning is available from:

American Planning Association
  1776 Massachusetts Avenue, NW
  Washington, DC 20036

Association of Collegiate Schools of Planning
  College of Design, Architecture, Art, and Planning
  University of Cincinnati
  Cincinnati, OH 45221

CHAPTER 6

CAREERS IN POLITICAL SCIENCE AND ECONOMICS

In this chapter, career opportunities in political science and economics are discussed. Included in this chapter is an overview of the career opportunities in statistics, a field of study whose techniques are used extensively by political scientists and economists.

POLITICAL SCIENCE

Political science is the study of politics, governments, and the political process. It focuses on how governments make decisions and investigates the content, implementation, and effects of those decisions.

Political scientists study all aspects of political behavior, such as the origin, development, and interrelationships of political institutions. They formulate and develop political theory. They conduct research and analyze and interpret the results of their studies. They then prepare reports that detail their findings, make recommendations, and form conclusions.

The world and its problems are both the main concern and the principal laboratory of the modern political scientist. Political scientists study the political behavior of people, groups, and nations in an effort to understand why they behave as they do, to predict what they will do next, and sometimes to suggest how they should behave in the future.

Political scientists also study government and its institutions, including city councils, state legislatures, national assemblies, political parties, public policies, and the relationships among nations and groups.

Political science goes beyond even these topics to include the study of class systems, pressure groups, the nature of power, and the psychology of leadership. Political scientists investigate the ways in which people organize, distribute, and use political power.

Political science is the study of the process of government. The scope of the science ranges from international organizations such as the United Nations to meetings of the local school board.

Political scientists study such topics as public opinion and ideologies or belief systems. They analyze the structure and operation of groups that have power.

Political scientists use many methods to obtain information. They conduct public surveys, analyze the results of elections, and interpret public documents. The discipline of political science applies statistical procedures. Its researchers use computers to manage and process extremely large amounts of data.

MAJOR CAREERS IN POLITICAL SCIENCE

Political science graduates are involved in the kinds of work for which political science expertise has always been important—federal, state, and local government; law; politics; foreign service; and public information. Political scientists employed by federal, state, or local governments generally specialize in one or two policy areas. Frequently, they work with quantitative data.

Teaching and Research

Most political scientists work in colleges and universities. There they are involved in teaching and research.

Business

One-third of political science graduates find employment in the business sector. After employment, some receive special training in areas including policy analysis and consumer affairs.

Labor Relations Managers

Labor relations managers are in charge of the hourly employee relations program of the firm. They analyze collective bargaining agreements and assist management in developing and applying labor relations policies and practices. Labor relations managers also represent management in investigating and settling grievances. They are employed by business, industry, and consulting firms.

Politics

Some political science graduates are involved in politics as candidates, appointees, or campaign consultants.

Legislative Assistants

Legislative assistants work with legislators in preparing new legislation. They analyze policy issues and speak with lobbyists, voters, and members of the press on behalf of the legislators. They also may assist with campaign activities.

Foreign Service

Foreign service officers represent the government of the United States in diplomatic or consular posts abroad. They also assist citizens of the United States in the host country. They are employed by the State Department.

Media

Political science graduates are employed as analysts, political writers, and commentators by newspapers and magazines and radio and television stations.

Law

Many of those who study political science select careers in the legal profession. Paralegal assistants are employed by lawyers. Paralegals, who are trained assistants to lawyers, belong to the fastest-growing profession in the United States. According to the U.S. Bureau of Labor Statistics, paralegals number well over fifty thousand nationwide and will at least double in number in the next decade. Paralegal assistants research law, investigate facts, and prepare legal documents. They maintain document files and take inventory of the client's personal property in estate planning.

Lawyers conduct civil and criminal lawsuits, prepare legal documents, and advise their clients. They gather evidence in civil and criminal cases and represent their clients in court or at government hearings.

Corporate lawyers represent large corporations. They advise management of their legal rights and obligations. They are employed by private businesses and industries.

Probate lawyers specialize in estate settlement and planning. They draft wills and deeds of trust for their clients. Many probate lawyers are self-employed.

Judges administer the judicial system. They settle disputes, examine evidence, and instruct juries in laws and legal procedures. They sentence defendants in criminal cases and decide settlements in civil cases. Judges are politically appointed or elected and work in federal, state, county, or municipal governments.

RELATED CAREERS

Careers related to political science include public administration, urban and regional planning, law enforcement, systems analysis, and legal administration. New fields opening up for political science graduates include environmental control and criminal justice and corrections.

It is also helpful to have political science training for jobs in journalism, business, and industry. This is particularly true of businesses and industries that deal with the government or have international operations.

EMPLOYMENT OPPORTUNITIES

The greatest opportunities for political science graduates exist for those with mastery of a specialized or important policy area. The ability to work effectively with statistics, computers, data analysis, and written English is extremely valuable.

The best positions for political science instructors will be found in major universities.

The employment potential for labor relations managers is expected to be stable through the next decade.

Job opportunities for legislative assistants are limited. Sites of the best opportunities are in the state capitals and Washington, D.C.

Competition for positions as foreign service officers is intense. Opportunities for employment are dependent upon the candidate's talent, determination, and good fortune.

The job market remains highly competitive for political science graduates entering journalism and radio and television. The best opportunities for advancement are in small or average-sized communities with a relatively small newspaper or station.

The legal job market is difficult to measure. However, the move toward legal service plans for the poor and middle class and the increasing complexity of governments and business suggest an increase in demand for legal services.

There will continue to be some demand for lawyers, but the increased number of law school graduates will result in greater competition. Prospects for establishing new law practices are best in smaller communities and suburban areas.

The best opportunities for corporate lawyers are in large metropolitan areas.

SALARIES AND EARNINGS

Starting salaries for bachelor's degree political scientists vary by qualifications and occupational areas but average $18,000.

The average beginning salary of labor relations managers is $29,500.

Foreign service officers' average starting salary is $29,000.

Political scientists employed as instructors in colleges and universities earn an average starting salary of $36,500.

The national average beginning salary of legislative assistants is $27,000.

Paralegal assistants earn a beginning average salary of $22,000. They earn 10 to 25 percent more for overtime work.

Law school graduates earn average beginning salaries ranging from $27,000 to $36,000. Experienced lawyers working outside of private practice average $90,000. The national average salary for beginning probate lawyers is $37,000. That of beginning corporate lawyers is $38,000. The average salary of judges is $57,000.

PREPARING FOR A CAREER
IN POLITICAL SCIENCE

High School Preparation

Courses that develop essential skills, such as the ability to write, read and analyze, think logically, and communicate orally, are extremely beneficial.

Courses in history, economics, and computer science are very useful. Since some positions with the government require fluency in a foreign language, early training is desirable.

Educational Requirements

For most careers in political science, a bachelor's degree is the minimum requirement. Some associate degree programs emphasize the knowledge, skills, and attitudes needed for jobs and career advancement in public service.

Paralegal assistants are generally required to have a bachelor's degree.

Lawyers must be graduates of law schools and be admitted to the bar. As undergraduates, they generally enroll in comprehensive programs that involve written and oral communication skills and critical and analytical thinking. A solid background in the social sciences, humanities, and business-related courses is strongly recommended.

Political scientists who are instructors at four-year colleges and universities generally must have a Ph.D.

SOURCES OF ADDITIONAL INFORMATION

For more information on careers in political science and allied fields, contact:

Academy of Political Science
  2852 Broadway Avenue
  New York, NY 10025

American Bar Association
  750 North Lake Shore Drive
  Chicago, IL 60611

American Colleges of Probate Counsel
  2716 Ocean Park Boulevard
  Suite 1080
  Santa Monica, CA 90405

American Corporate Counsel Association
  1225 Connecticut Avenue, NW
  Suite 202
  Washington, DC 20036

American Institute of Paralegal Studies
  1855 Fountain Square Court
  Suite 311
  Columbus, OH 43224

American Political Science Association
  1527 New Hampshire Avenue, NW
  Washington, DC 20036

American Society for Personnel Administration
  606 North Washington Street
  Alexandria, VA 22314

Association of American Law Schools
  Law School Admission Council
  One Dupont Circle, NW
  Suite 370
  Washington, DC 20036

Canadian Political Science Association
  #205 One Stewart Street
  Ottawa, ON K1N 6H7

Constitutional Rights Foundation
  1510 Coltner Avenue
  West Los Angeles, CA 90025

Foreign Policy Association
  205 Lexington Avenue
  New York, NY 10016

National Association for Law Placement
  Administrative Office
  440 First Street, NW
  Suite 302
  Washington, DC 20001

National Association of Schools and Public Affairs
     and Administration
   1120 G Street, NW
   Suite 520
   Washington, DC 20005

U.S. Department of State
   Recruitment Division
   P.O. Box 9317—Rosslyn Street
   Arlington, VA 22209

World Affairs Council of Philadelphia
   Student-Teacher Activities Department
   Third Floor Gallery
   The John Wanamaker Stores
   Thirteenth and Market Streets
   Philadelphia, PA 19107

World Policy Institute
   777 United Nations Plaza
   New York, NY 10017

ECONOMICS

Economists study the way we allocate our resources to produce a wide variety of goods and services. In other words, economists study how people with limited resources satisfy their wants and needs. They study the ways a society uses scarce resources, such as water, land, and fuel, to produce goods and services.

Economists investigate the causes and effects of world hunger, inflation, unemployment, and taxes. They study where we are, where we should be in the future, and how we can get there.

Almost all political, social, and industrial problems can be described in terms of the conflict that exists between a people's unlimited desire for higher living standards and the limited resources available to satisfy this desire. Economists try to help societies, governments, and businesses resolve this conflict.

MAJOR CAREERS IN ECONOMICS

People with degrees in economics work in business, government, education, and research. Economists conduct research to help interpret economic relationships. They suggest solutions for problems arising from the production and distribution of goods and services. Economists compile, review, and analyze data and then organize these data into reports. They formulate policies and recommend solutions for economic problems.

Government Economists

Many economists work for the government. Local, state, and national governments need economists to help establish public policy.

Government economists help make decisions on such important policy issues as to how to control inflation, how to lower unemployment, and how to design an efficient tax system. Some of the federal agencies that hire large staffs of economists are the departments of Commerce, Treasury, Labor, State, and Agriculture. Federal agencies that employ many economists include the Federal Reserve System, the President's Council of Economic Advisors, the Congressional Budget Office, and the Joint Economic Committee.

Business Economists

Economists may work in banks, trade associations, or consulting firms. Many large businesses and banks hire economists to forecast the course of economic events.

Business economists forecast the demand for products, analyze market conditions, and supply the basic financial information needed for successful long-range business planning. One-third of American economists work in business. They are employed by firms in manufacturing, transportation, and communications and by public utilities.

Teaching and Research

Jobs in universities, colleges, and research agencies challenge economics graduates to teach people the principles of economics and how to use them to solve problems. There is a steady demand for economics professors at colleges and universities.

Economists in research agencies analyze economic problems, suggest ways to solve them, and try to figure out how well the solutions work. They are involved in interdisciplinary work, which ranges in scope from the economics of urban problems to redesigning the international monetary system.

RELATED CAREERS

Careers closely allied to economics include those in economic geography or geology, urban and regional planning, political science, and accounting. Those with training in economics can be employed as systems analysts, financial analysts, investment consultants, insurance underwriters, and budget officers.

EMPLOYMENT OPPORTUNITIES

The number of economists will continue to grow at an average rate through the next decade with career opportunities in manufacturing, financial services, advertising agencies, research organizations, and consulting firms.

The best opportunities for economists are in government, financial institutions, and colleges and universities.

SALARIES AND EARNINGS

New assistant professors in colleges and universities earn about $47,500. Business entrants with bachelor's degrees earn about $27,500 annually. Those with master's degrees earn about $44,000. Salaries for entrants in the federal government range from $29,500 to $37,500 annually. Economists in business average about $70,000 annually. Those employed by the federal government earn about $57,000 annually.

PREPARING FOR A CAREER IN ECONOMICS

High School Preparation

Anyone considering a four-year major in economics should have a minimum of one year of high school algebra. A stronger high school background is preferred, including additional algebra and one year of plane geometry.

Educational Requirements

The title *economist* usually requires a graduate degree. A bachelor's degree in economics permits an individual to participate in entry-level training programs. For most positions, graduate training is preferred or required.

SOURCES OF ADDITIONAL INFORMATION

For more information about careers in economics, contact:

The American Economic Association
   1313 Twenty-first Avenue, South
   Suite 809
   Nashville, TN 37212

Canadian Economics Association
   Stephen Leacock Bldg.
   Department of Economics
   McGill University
   855, Rue Sherbrooke Ouest
   Montreal, PQ H3A 2T7

Foundation for Economic Education
   30 South Broadway Avenue
   Irvington, NY 10533

Joint Council on Economic Education
   1212 Avenue of the Americas
   New York, NY 10036

National Association of Business Economists
   28349 Chagrin Boulevard
   Suite 201
   Cleveland, OH 44122

National Economist Club
  P.O. Box 19381
  Washington, DC 20036

Overseas Development Council
  1717 Massachusetts Avenue, NW
  Washington, DC 20036

STATISTICS AND THE SOCIAL SCIENCES

Statistics deals with the collection, analysis, and reporting of information. Statisticians deal with numerical data. That is, they try to make sense out of numbers. They draw valid conclusions after weighing the evidence. They match data with problems. They decide what information to collect and how. They then try to predict future developments.

Statistics are used every day. From the batting averages of major league baseball players to how four out of five doctors feel about a painkiller, statistics invade our everyday life now more than ever. Statistics are used in all areas of education, industry, and government.

Many social scientists use statistical methods in their research. For example, they may use them to predict population growth, economic conditions, and voting patterns. Sometimes, a statistician who is working with data concerning voting patterns also may be called a political scientist.

MAJOR CAREERS IN STATISTICS

In 1996, statisticians held about twenty thousand jobs. Most of these positions were in business and industry. The remaining jobs were in government. Most of them were in federal agencies or offices.

EMPLOYMENT OPPORTUNITIES

Employment opportunities for those who combine training in an applied field and statistics are expected to be favorable through the 1990s. Private industry will need more statisticians in many areas. All levels of government agencies—federal, state, and local—will need statisticians in fields such as population studies, transportation, energy conservation, and consumer surveys.

Those who hold graduate degrees have even better employment opportunities. There is a real need in colleges and universities for statisticians who have completed a doctoral degree.

SALARIES AND EARNINGS

The data concerning salaries of statisticians in private industry are limited. In government, the salary data are more complete.

The annual starting salary for those who hold a bachelor's degree ranges from about $19,000 to $23,500. The amount is determined by the person's college grades.

Statisticians with a master's degree earn between $27,000 and $31,000. Those with a doctoral degree earn a beginning salary of approximately $35,000.

EDUCATIONAL REQUIREMENTS

A bachelor's degree with a major in mathematics or statistics is required for many entry-level jobs in statistics. Other positions do not require a degree with a major in statistics. In fact, some employers prefer someone who has a bachelor's degree in an applied field, such as economics, and a minor in statistics.

Applicants for jobs in statistics must have training in several areas. Included are courses in mathematics through calculus, statistical method, and probability theory. A strong background in computer science also is especially recommended.

SOURCES OF ADDITIONAL INFORMATION

More information about careers in the field of statistics is available from:

American Statistical Association
  1429 Duke Avenue
  Alexandria, VA 22314

Institute of Mathematical Statistics
  3401 Investment Boulevard, No. 7
  Hayward, CA 94545

CHAPTER 7

TEACHING AND
THE SOCIAL SCIENCES

One of the astronauts killed in the 1986 space shuttle Challenger disaster was Christa McAuliffe, a secondary school social studies teacher. She once said, "I shape the future. I teach." Although this statement could describe a teacher of any subject, it is particularly appropriate for one who chooses to teach social studies.

David Armstrong, a professor at Texas A & M University, writes that in some respects, a social studies teacher is like a ninety-year-old man planting an oak tree in his front yard. He must till the soil, knowing that he may never see the tree (or, in the teacher's case, the student) in a state of full and mature glory.

Social studies teachers believe in the future. They teach, knowing that their influence on their students can compete successfully with other influences that shape them. Realizing this, social studies teachers "plant," knowing that it is their students who will determine the nature of the harvest.

THE SOCIAL STUDIES IN ELEMENTARY
AND SECONDARY SCHOOLS

Social studies is an offspring of the social sciences. In other words, the social sciences can be described as the parent disciplines of social studies. Social studies is a basic subject in the elementary and secondary school curriculum. According to the National Council for the Social Studies, the premier professional organization for social studies teachers, social studies draws its subject matter content primarily from history, the social sciences, and, in some respects, from the humanities and science.

Classroom instruction in social studies focuses on these areas of knowledge:

- the history and culture of the United States and the world
- physical, political, economic, and cultural geography
- theories, systems, structures, and processes of both government and economics
- the individual, group, community, and society; intergroup and interpersonal relationships
- global relationships between and among nations, races, cultures, and institutions

According to the National Council for the Social Studies, exemplary programs in social studies use this knowledge base to teach skills, concepts, and generalizations that can help students "understand the sweep of human affairs and ways of managing conflict consistent with democratic procedures."

In the United States, there are three levels of education: elementary, secondary, and postsecondary. The necessary skills, required educational training, and desired personal traits of the teachers at each level vary.

Teaching in the Elementary School

Elementary teachers instruct pupils in grades kindergarten through six. The educational requirements for elementary teachers are general rather than specific because they are responsible for teaching several subjects to these young students.

In most elementary schools, the teachers work with the same students during the entire school day. In some elementary schools, the teachers in intermediate grades four through six form instructional teams.

They divide the chief academic subjects among them. One teacher then teaches all three science classes, another teaches three math classes, and the third teaches social studies to all the students enrolled in grades four, five, and six. Depending on the structure of the individual elementary school, this instructional approach is called departmentalization or team teaching.

Effective elementary school teachers enjoy being with children. They realize that they play a critical role in their pupils' individual development.

Elementary school teachers are concerned with the intellectual growth and general well-being of their pupils. They are responsible for teaching large groups of students, evaluating pupil progress, maintaining pupil records, and providing a secure learning environment. They teach as many as eight different subjects, such as math, language, arts, and science. One of the most important subject areas they teach is social studies.

Elementary School Social Studies

The social studies curriculum in the lower primary grades, kindergarten through two, draws much of its content from the disciplines of sociology and psychology. The children learn about themselves, their homes and families, and their neighborhoods. They learn about emotions, such as anger and jealousy, and socially acceptable ways to handle them.

In the third and fourth grades, the pupils generally study their local community and state. They learn about their history, geography, government, and culture. They investigate how needs and wants are satisfied by the people who live there and how groups work together to improve the quality of life in their community and state.

In the fifth and sixth grades of elementary school, the pupils learn about the United States and other countries in the world. They focus on American history and geography and examine our nation's roots in other cultures and civilizations. They learn about global awareness and worldwide interdependence.

Requirements for Teaching
Elementary School Social Studies

Licensing of teachers in the United States is the responsibility of the individual states. Although certification requirements vary, an elementary school teacher is generally authorized to teach all subject areas, grades kindergarten through six. Information about each state's licensing requirements can be obtained from the teacher certification office of that state. A listing of teacher certification offices of the fifty states, District of Columbia, Puerto Rico, and the American Virgin Islands is provided in Appendix A. Appendix B lists the teacher certification offices of Canada's provinces and territories.

Teaching in the Secondary School

Secondary school teachers work with pupils in grades seven through twelve. They help their students move from childhood to adulthood. Unlike the elementary school teachers, who teach many subject areas to the same groups of students, secondary school teachers specialize in subject matter fields. They may teach related subjects such as American history and government classes, but they must be licensed in each subject area they teach.

Effective secondary school teachers enjoy working with adolescents and young adults. They not only teach their students about their areas of specialization, but they frequently also help them with personal and academic problems. One of the important activities they perform is assisting their students as they choose their careers or select schools for additional training or education.

Secondary School Social Studies

The vast majority of high schools offer courses in history and geography. In most states, study in these two areas is a requirement for high school graduation. In many states, semester-long courses in political science and, less frequently, economics are also requisites for a high school diploma. Courses in psychology, anthropology, and sociology are generally elective courses and, accordingly, few in number.

The school social studies curriculum has been the focus of several recent studies. Many educated Americans deplore a low level of knowledge in history, geography, and economics among high school students.

A widely received report on the status of history in American schools was issued in 1988 by the Bradley Commission. This commission, chaired by Kenneth Jackson, Mellon professor of history and the social sciences at Columbia University, was established in 1987 through a grant from the Lynde and Harry Bradley Foundation of Milwaukee.

The Bradley Commission was composed of seventeen scholars and teachers, including three Pulitzer Prize–winning historians. It harshly criticized the history curriculum in the nation's schools and called for required studies in history for all students, whether or not they are preparing for college.

The commission urged that history be required of all students because no matter what career they choose, they will all be citizens. They must, then, have an opportunity to learn American, European, and world history and geography throughout their school years.

The social studies curriculum of secondary schools is being examined by many scholars and educators. It is very likely that state requirements for graduation will be included in this examination process.

Requirements for Teaching
Secondary School Social Studies

During the last several years, several significant efforts have been made to enhance the qualifications of teachers in the United States. Some states now require an internship for beginning teachers and the successful completion of competency exams prior to certification.

Several states have abolished teacher-education majors in their state institutions. Those who intend to teach in grades seven through twelve are required to complete a baccalaureate degree in the specific discipline. For example, if someone intends to teach economics in high school, a bachelor's degree in economics is required.

The requirements for teacher certification are undergoing scrutiny in many states. Thus, it is advisable to contact the certification office of the state in which employment as a teacher is sought.

A listing of the certification offices of the fifty states, the American Virgin Islands, Puerto Rico, and the District of Columbia is provided in Appendix A. A listing of the teacher certification offices in the Canadian provinces and territories is listed in Appendix B.

REQUIREMENTS FOR TEACHERS

All states require a baccalaureate degree for initial licensure as a teacher. In several states, additional course work or a graduate degree is required for continued certification. All studies must be completed at an accredited college or university.

A list of colleges and universities accredited by the National Council for Accreditation of Teacher Education (NCATE) can be obtained from:

National Council for Accreditation of Teacher Education
    1919 Pennsylvania Avenue, NW
    Suite 202
    Washington, DC 20006

Student Teaching

The interest of the American people in having their teachers certified is considerably older than their interest in having them well trained. Even during colonial times, it was customary for public officials to examine candidates for employment as teachers.

Later, the states utilized certification as a positive instrument to ensure the quality of teachers. Public officials accordingly granted different types of teaching certificates, proportioning their duration to the amount of training taken to receive them.

More recently, differentiation in the certificates issued to teachers took a different direction. Instead of certifying competence to teach for a certain length of time, the state then began to certify competence in a particular field of teaching.

Such specialization in certification was evidence of the technical complexity that the professional study of education has achieved in the twentieth century. By World War II, neither competence in educational technique nor mastery of subject matter was regarded as sufficient to qualify for teaching in America's schools.

Rigorous rules of certification defined requirements in both. In additional to subject-matter specialization, they required at least courses in educational psychology and principles of education and a specified number of hours spent in practice teaching.

In most four-year colleges, student teaching occurs near the end of the program. Student teaching programs last from eight to sixteen weeks. During that time, the student teacher works closely with an experienced teacher in the classroom. The student teacher's responsibilities gradually increase from observing, assisting, and practicing to teaching a full day.

The student teacher's progress is evaluated by the classroom teacher and by a representative of the university granting the teaching degree.

Many educators regard the student teaching experience as the best predictor of the future teacher's performance. It is, in fact, the final stage of the student's undergraduate education.

In order to student teach, many states require a specific grade point average in college course work. In addition to knowing what to teach, secondary school teachers must be able to communicate with their students. They must also know how to help the students learn. These skills are among those evaluated during the student-teaching experience.

Teacher Examinations

In all states, prospective teachers must successfully complete the undergraduate program including student teaching. In many states, additional requirements must be met before prospective teachers can be certified. Chief among these additional requirements is a program of testing or evaluating the prospective teachers. Tests are administered in these areas:

- Basic skills—proficiency in writing, reading, spelling, and math
- Subject matter—mastery of the material to be taught
- Teaching skills—understanding of general principles of learning and education; social and cultural forces that influence curriculum and teaching; organization and legal bases of education.

Initial Certification

Upon completion of the baccalaureate program, competency tests, and certification requirements, the candidate receives an initial teaching certificate.

In several states, the newly certified teacher must then serve a year's internship in an accredited school. The beginning teacher has a full-day teaching assignment and receives regular pay and benefits.

An outstanding experienced teacher, who also has a full-time teaching assignment, serves as the beginning teacher's mentor. The mentor meets with the beginning teacher on a regular basis and provides guidance and support during the critical first year of teaching.

Subsequent Certification

Almost all states require additional training or education for the renewal of the teaching certificate. Many states require a graduate degree. To obtain information about the requirements for renewed certification, write to the appropriate certification officers listed in Appendix A.

TEACHERS' SALARIES

In *High School,* the critically acclaimed report on secondary education in America, author Ernest Boyer states that the United States has always been ambivalent about teachers. He quotes Professor Lortie of the University of Chicago who wrote that "teaching is honored and disdained." It is praised as "dedicated service" and lampooned as "easy work." Teaching from its beginnings has held a special, but shadowed, social standing. Real regard shown for those who teach has never matched professed regard.

Boyer claims that teaching today occupies an even more "shadowed place" in the public's esteem with a greater percentage of parents still preferring that their children not become teachers in U.S. public schools.

Combined with this negative public image toward teachers are other factors that make a career in teaching a less desirable choice. Teacher salaries for the most part neither reflect the years of education needed to become a teacher nor adequately reward outstanding teachers for their performance.

It must be noted that some advances in teacher salaries are being made. Nonetheless, the salaries for many beginning teachers today are less than $25,000.

In many schools, teachers receive additional pay for coaching sports and working with students in extracurricular activities such as drama club and speech teams.

TEACHER SUPPLY AND DEMAND

The need for new teachers is difficult to determine. The National Center for Education Statistics projects that the demand for teachers will increase for the immediate future. This increased need for new teachers is the result of several factors, which include changes in enrollment, changes in school programs that affect the pupil-teacher ratio, and teacher turnover or retirement.

The Association for School, College, and University Staffing (ASCUS) has been involved in the assessment of teacher supply and demand since the early 1970s. The research reports compiled by ASCUS provide accurate, valuable data for prospective teachers. Copies of the annual ASCUS reports are generally available at colleges and universities.

Another source that will aid prospective teachers is *Patterson's American Education,* published by Educational

Directories, Inc. This guide identifies all school districts in the United States and lists all senior and junior high schools. It also provides the name of each district's superintendent and address. *Patterson's American Education* is revised annually and is available in many large libraries.

An excellent resource for prospective social studies teachers is the National Council for the Social Studies (NCSS). Its address is 3615 Wisconsin Avenue, NW, Washington, D.C., 20016. NCSS is the preeminent professional organization for social studies educators. Its journal, *Social Education,* is its major publication.

HIGH SCHOOL PREPARATION

To be a social studies teacher requires effective oral and written communication skills and knowledge of the subject matter to be taught.

Your high school preparation should include courses in academic English, the social sciences, and a foreign language.

It would be advantageous, also, to join your local chapter of Future Teachers of America. You might also choose to serve as a volunteer, assisting teachers in your district or tutoring students having difficulty in a course in which you perform well.

If you intend to work after school, try to select positions that enable you to work with people. These experiences will be valuable ones as you pursue your goal.

You are, after all, intending to enter a noble profession. An ancient proverb reads:

> Give a man a fish and you feed him today. Teach a man how to fish and you feed him for a lifetime.

Teaching is like that. It looks to the future and attempts to empower the learner to strive for the very best.

TEACHING THE SOCIAL SCIENCES IN COLLEGES AND UNIVERSITIES

College and university faculty teach undergraduate students, graduate students, or both. They prepare and give lectures in their areas of specialization and evaluate their students' progress. Faculty in the social sciences at major universities are expected to conduct scholarly research in their fields and report their findings. Many institutions require the publication of research for advancement.

According to the Census Bureau, more than twelve million full-time and part-time students are enrolled in the nation's colleges and universities. The faculty of those institutions teach and advise them. In 1994, college and university faculty members held about 823,000 positions in

American institutions. Over 70 percent of these institutions were public ones, that is, supported by the state.

Most four-year colleges require their faculty members to hold a doctoral degree for advancement. Doctoral programs require several years of full-time study beyond the bachelor's degree. Doctoral programs include twenty or more courses that are increasingly specialized in the area of study. A series of comprehensive examinations is also part of a doctoral program. The final stage is the successful completion of the doctoral dissertation, which is a report of original research in the field. The dissertation, completed under the guidance of a faculty adviser, usually requires one or two years of full-time work.

Some four-year colleges will hire a doctoral student who has completed all the course work but not the dissertation. This faculty member is frequently described as A.B.D. (all but dissertation) and is generally required to complete it during a time stipulated at employment. In two-year colleges, the doctorate is helpful but generally not required.

Tenure and Rank

An important step in a faculty member's academic career is tenure. With tenure, a faculty member cannot ordinarily be fired. If tenure is denied, the faculty member usually must leave the institution.

Tenure is granted after a period of rigorous evaluation. New faculty members are hired generally without tenure.

Only after a probationary period of up to seven years are they recommended by their academic departments for tenure. This recommendation is based on a critical review of their records as teachers and researchers and their other contributions to the university.

Advancement in the university is determined by these and other contributions made by the faculty member. There are four levels of advancement for faculty members. Recommendations for promotion usually begin with positive evaluations by senior faculty members in the academic department.

Instructors are usually those who are hired A.B.D. They generally teach twelve to fourteen hours each week. They instruct only undergraduates who are enrolled in introductory level courses.

Assistant professors usually have completed all requirements for the doctorate. They teach about twelve hours each week and frequently are responsible for larger classes of undergraduate students. They must also be involved in research and publication, especially if they hope to receive tenure.

Associate professors teach an average of nine hours each week. They are frequently assigned upper-division courses and selected graduate courses. The rank of associate professor is almost always a tenured position.

Full professors hold the highest academic rank of the faculty in a college or university. At many colleges and universities, they teach only one or two classes each week. They also supervise doctoral students who are completing their dissertations. The rank of professor is increasingly difficult to attain. Promotion is increasingly based only on the faculty member's publications, research, and reputation as a scholar.

Faculty Salaries

Earnings vary according to faculty rank and type of institution and, in some cases, by field. Faculty in 4-year institutions earn higher salaries, on the average, than those in 2-year schools. According to a 1994–1995 survey by the American Association of University Professors, salaries for full-time faculty on 9-month contracts averaged $49,500. By rank, the average for professors was $63,500; associate professors, $47,000; assistant professors, $39,100; lecturers, $32,600; and instructors, $29,700. Those on 11- or 12-month contracts obviously earned more.

Many faculty members have added earnings, both during the academic year and the summer, from consulting, teaching additional courses, research, writing for publication, or other employment.

Job Outlook

According to the *Occupational Outlook Handbook,* employment of college and university faculty is expected to increase about as fast as the average for all occupations through the year 2005 as enrollments in higher education increase. Many additional openings will arise as faculty members retire. Faculty retirements should increase significantly from the late 1990s through 2005 as a large number of faculty who entered the profession during the 1950s and 1960s reach retirement age. Most faculty members likely to retire are full-time tenured professors. However, in an effort to cut costs, institutions are expected to either leave many of these positions vacant or hire part-time faculty members as replacements. Prospective job applicants should be prepared to face intense competition for available jobs as growing numbers of Ph.D. graduates vie for fewer full-time openings.

Enrollments in institutions of higher education increased in the 1980s and early 1990s despite a decline in the traditional college-age (18–24) population. This resulted from a higher proportion of 18- to 24-year olds attending college, along with a growing number of part-time, female, and older students. Enrollments are expected to continue to grow through the year 2005, particularly as the traditional college-age population begins increasing after 1996, when the leading edge of the baby-boom "echo" generation (children of the baby boomers) reaches college age.

In the past two decades, keen competition for faculty jobs forced some applicants to accept part-time or short-term academic appointments that offered little hope of tenure, and others to seek nonacademic positions. This trend of hiring adjunct or part-time faculty is likely to continue due to financial difficulties faced by colleges and universities.

Many states have reduced funding for higher education. As a result, colleges have increased the hiring of part-time faculty to save money on pay and benefits. With uncertainty over future funding, many colleges and universities are taking steps to cut costs. They are emphasizing certain academic programs while eliminating others, increasing class size, stepping up fundraising efforts, and closely monitoring expenses.

Once enrollments and retirements start increasing at a faster pace in the late 1990s, opportunities for college faculty positions may begin to improve somewhat.

SOURCES OF ADDITIONAL INFORMATION

For further information, contact:

American Association of University Professors
  1012 Fourteenth Street, NW
  Suite 500
  Washington, DC 20005

Consortium of Social Science Associations
  1200 Seventeenth Street, NW
  Suite 520
  Washington, DC 20036

Additional information is also available from the professional societies for the respective academic discipline. A listing of these societies is provided in the earlier chapters on the seven social science disciplines.

CHAPTER 8

A FINAL LOOK AT SOCIAL SCIENCE CAREERS

OVERVIEW OF THE SOCIAL SCIENCES

Social scientists study how people and societies work. Though the number of social scientists in the United States is not proportionately large, the importance of their disciplines should not be minimized. All of us use the content of the social sciences to improve our understanding of other people and their behavior.

The principles of the social sciences are all around us. We use them in many aspects of our personal and social lives. An examination of the contents of a daily newspaper can illustrate this.

The headlines and stories on page one are frequently concerned with conflicts, wars, crime, and the economy. Principles and content from political science, history, geography, economics, and sociology are an integral part of these daily news reports.

The classified ads list items to be bought and sold. They list jobs available or wanted. Both these activities involve the social science of economics.

The sports pages are more easily understood when the reader understands principles of psychology, geography, economics, and statistics.

The travel section is concerned with geography, anthropology, and history; the financial pages with economics. Sections on leisure activities frequently involve principles from sociology, anthropology, and psychology. The obituaries are concerned with history, sociology, and anthropology. The comic pages clearly involve psychology, sociology, and anthropology.

Yet many of us read the daily newspaper, not realizing that its features represent the social science disciplines.

Even if you do not choose a career in the social sciences, their study will enhance your understanding of the world around you.

CAREER PREREQUISITES

The *Occupational Outlook Quarterly* noted that there are certain requirements for those choosing careers in the social sciences. Social science careers require persons who have flexibility in thinking, an interest in problem solving, an ability to listen, and a willingness to ask questions.

The editors of the *Occupational Outlook Quarterly* note that the amount and time of training in the social sciences vary for different careers. Some careers require great human understanding and two years of college. Others require advanced graduate degrees in the appropriate field of studies. You should remember that most positions in the social sciences require at least a master's degree.

You must then know how to study. You should also take appropriate courses in high school.

A strong academic program is recommended. In 1983, the Reagan administration issued a report called *A Nation at Risk*. It identified the poor condition of education in America's elementary and secondary schools. This report prompted state legislatures to introduce several measures intended to improve the quality of the education of teachers. This report was reaffirmed by Presidents Bush and Clinton and during the latter's administration, *Goals 2000* was emphasized.

Some state legislatures examined other aspects of education. They tightened the requirements for admission to their public colleges and universities. In Ohio, for example, high school graduates are unconditionally admitted to the state's institutions only if they have successfully completed an academic program in high school. This means that a series of courses in mathematics, science, English, and the social sciences must have been part of the students' curriculum.

In 1983, the College Board published an outstanding booklet, *Academic Preparation for College: What Students Need to Know and Be Able to Do.* This booklet is part of a project begun in 1980 by the College Board. It was intended "to strengthen the academic quality of secondary education and to ensure equality of opportunity for postsecondary education for all students."

Academic Preparation for College lists and describes the knowledge and skills needed by all prospective college students. According to the College Board, the basic academic competencies are reading, writing, speaking and listening, mathematics, reasoning, and studying. These competencies or acquired skills are closely related to the basic academic subjects. Without them, knowing the concepts of history, science, language, and other academic subjects is impossible.

One of the basic academic subjects taught and studied in American high schools is social studies. This subject area focuses on the complexity of our social environment. Social studies combines the study of history and the social sciences and promotes skills in citizenship.

The successful completion of high school courses in the social studies will prepare college entrants for advanced work in history and the social sciences including geography, anthropology, sociology, political science, psychology, and economics.

The College Board recommends that those planning to enter college also study a foreign language. The merits of knowing another language are significant. It fosters a greater awareness of the similarities and differences among the cultures in the world. Those who know a foreign language can more readily appreciate other people's values and ways of life. Knowledge of a foreign language helps students prepare for careers in commerce, international relations, law, and the arts. College entrants need a background in another language to pursue advanced degrees in fields such as history.

If you choose to pursue a career in one of the social sciences, you should also be able to use a computer. Today it is a basic tool for acquiring knowledge, organizing systems, and solving problems. As such, the computer is having a real and profound effect on learning and the world of work. It is used extensively by many social scientists.

A solid preparation in high school will be of great worth to those entering college. Courses like those described above will help the students bound for college in several important activities. Included are these:

- Gathering, assessing, and processing information
- Understanding the concepts of space and time
- Recognizing the importance of the social sciences and humanities to the past, present, and future

- Communicating and cooperating with others
- Applying problem-solving skills and critical thinking to personal and social issues

With this strong academic background from high school, you are well prepared to begin working toward a career in the social sciences. There is, however, one other step you can take.

To help you find out if you are indeed suited for a career in the social sciences, many counselors recommend you try to get some practical work experience in a related field. The *Occupational Outlook Quarterly* suggests volunteering in hospitals, museums, schools, and libraries. Summer and part-time jobs working with people also can be extremely helpful.

CAREERS AND THE SOCIAL SCIENCES

Most employers realize that their employees are much more productive when they are happy in their work. Effective managers and corporations investigate and pursue ways to enhance their employees' job satisfaction. One of the outstanding programs to accomplish this includes a software package, Career Point 2, produced by Creative Systems Incorporated.*

---

*Information provided by Joanne J. Jorz, Creative Systems, 1010 Wayne Avenue, Suite 1420, Silver Spring, Maryland 20910.

Career Point 2 lists these facts about careers:

- Currently, people average ten jobs and three careers over their lifetime. Those entering the workforce today will have about fourteen jobs and four careers during their lifetime.
- Service industries will create all of the new jobs and most of the new wealth from now until the year 2000. Included in service industries are jobs in communications, finance, medical care, and high technology.
- By the year 2000, 47 percent of the workforce will be women. Sixty-one percent of the women in the United States will be at work outside the home.
- The average age of the workforce will be thirty-six by the year 2000. This is six years older than the average at any other time in U.S. history.
- Of all the new jobs that will be created by the year 2000, more than one-half will require some education beyond high school. Almost one-third of these jobs will be filled by college graduates.
- Fewer well-educated workers will be available in the year 2000 than in the 1960s and 1970s. But the number of jobs requiring higher skills will increase. This may cause employers to pay more to the well educated.

Therefore, planning for your future means surviving in a changing workplace. A career is something you can control. It is the lifelong sequence of jobs you hold. It is only one part of your life, but it has a significant impact on other life roles, such as spouse and parent.

Career Point 2 identifies four major steps in career development.

1. Looking at yourself to determine your strengths
2. Checking what you find against reality
3. Exploring many options
4. Setting goals and taking action

By following these steps, you will make better career decisions.

CHOOSING A COLLEGE OR UNIVERSITY

Choosing a college to attend is a major decision. It is affected by factors such as cost and distance from home. It is also affected by the perceived strengths of the school itself.

Here are some questions that you might consider when selecting a college or university:

Do Admissions Standards Vary for Different Groups? "Sliding" admission standards can make entry at prestigious schools easier for students in some groups. The following example of average freshman SAT scores at an ivy league university shows this variance.

Average	1350
Asian Americans	1350
Children of alumni	1280
Athletes	1240
Development cases (those with wealthy parents)	1220
African Americans	1200
Hispanics	1180

Do Standards Vary Among Different Colleges or Schools within the Same University? For example, are the admission standards the same for those majoring in architecture as they are for those majoring in general studies? The answer can indicate how quality-conscious a program is.

Can Students Take the Courses They Want and Need? Limited enrollment courses can wreck students' class schedules. Lists of such courses and the number of students allowed are often not published. Ask about them anyway.

Who Does the Teaching? In descending order of rank, college teachers are professors, associate professors, assistant professors, instructors, and teaching or graduate assistants. Find out how many hours teachers at different ranks spend in the classroom and whether teachers in high ranks teach freshman or survey courses. The answer can help indicate how much high-level attention students receive from faculty.

How Much Can the Library Be Used? This is not the same as, "How many volumes are in the library?" Some indications of how many students do, and can, use the library are the number of study carrels assigned to undergraduates and the number reserved for seniors' use only.

How Are Computers Used? Find out if personal computers are required. Learn if they are accessible to all students in open computer labs. Ask if there is easy access to the mainframe. Find out how many computers are available for student use.

What Is the Success Rate of Recent Alumni? This is not just the number who entered law or medical school. It should include the range and median scores of undergraduates who applied to graduate schools and how many applied but did not get admitted. You should also ask about the number of graduates who are employed after graduation. Find out how long it took them to get their jobs, if they are working in jobs related to their fields, and if they feel satisfied with the education they received.

Most importantly, you should visit the campus. After all, you may live and study there for several years. Talk with students, particularly those who are studying in the field in which you wish to major. If possible, spend a night on campus in a residence hall. Adequate pre-enrollment research will help prevent uninformed or poor decisions.

CONCLUSION

A career that focuses on individuals and their societies can be an extremely fulfilling one. Those who choose a career in one of the social sciences usually find much satisfaction in their choice. They are, after all, striving to be truly human.

OFFICES OF TEACHER CERTIFICATION IN THE UNITED STATES AND ITS TERRITORIES

Alabama

Coordinator of Teacher Certification Section
State Department of Education
349 State Office Building
Montgomery, AL 36130

Alaska

Coordinator of Teacher Education and Certification
State Department of Education
P.O. Box F
Juneau, AK 99811

Arizona

Arizona Department of Education
Teacher Certification Unit
1535 West Jefferson, Box 25609
Phoenix, AZ 85007

Arkansas

Arkansas Department of Education
  Teacher Education and Certification
  State Capitol Mall, Room 107-B
  Little Rock, AR 72201

California

Commission on Teacher Credentialing
  Licensing Branch
  Box 944270
  Sacramento, CA 94244

Colorado

Colorado Department of Education Teacher Certification
  201 East Colfax Avenue
  Denver, CO 80203

Connecticut

Bureau of Certification and Accreditation
  State Department of Education
  P.O. Box 2219
  Hartford, CT 06145

Delaware

Supervisor of Certification and Education
  State Department of Public Instruction
  Townsend Building
  P.O. Box 1402
  Dover, DE 19903

District of Columbia

Director of Certification and Accreditation
  District of Columbia Public Schools
  Suite 1004, 415 Twelfth Street, NW
  Washington, DC 20004

Florida

Florida Department of Education
  Commissioner of Education
  Teacher Certification
  Tallahassee, FL 32399

Georgia

Director of Certification
  Georgia Department of Education
  1425 Twin Towers East
  Atlanta, GA 30334

Hawaii

Administrator (Certification)
  Office of Personnel Services
  State Department of Education
  P.O. Box 2360
  Honolulu, HI 96804

Idaho

Director of Teacher Certification and Related Services
  State Department of Education
  Len B. Jordan Office Building
  650 West State
  Boise, ID 83720

Illinois

Manager, Teacher Certification and Placement
  Illinois State Board of Education
  100 North First Street
  Springfield, IL 62777

Iowa

Bureau of Teacher Education and Certification
  Department of Education
  Grimes State Office Building
  Des Moines, IA 50319-0146

Kansas

Director, Certification Section
  State Department of Education
  120 East Tenth Street
  Topeka, KS 66612

Kentucky

Director, Division of Teacher Education
    and Certification
  State Department of Education
  Capitol Plaza Tower
  Frankfort, KY 40601

Louisiana

Director, Higher Education
    and Teacher Certification, DOE
  P.O. Box 94064
  Baton Rouge, LA 70804

Maine

Director, Teacher Certification and Placement
  Department of Educational and Cultural Services
  State House, Station 23
  Augusta, ME 04333

Maryland

Maryland State Department of Education
  2000 West Baltimore Street
  Baltimore, MD 21201

Massachusetts

Director, Bureau of Teacher Preparation Certification
    and Placement
  Quincy Hancock Street
  Quincy, MA 02169

Michigan

Director, Division of Teacher Preparation
    Certification Services
  State Department of Education
  P.O. Box 30008
  Lansing, MI 48909

Minnesota

Manager, Personnel Licensing and Placement
  State Department of Education
  616 Capitol Square Building
  550 Cedar Street
  St. Paul, MN 55101

Mississippi

Office of Teacher Certification
  State Department of Education
  P.O. Box 771
  Jackson, MS 39205

Missouri

Director of Teacher Certification
  P.O. Box 480
  Jefferson City, MO 65102

Montana

Director of Teacher Certification
  Office of Public Instruction
  State Capitol
  Helena, MT 59620

Nebraska

Director of Teacher Education and Certification
  State Department of Education
  301 Centennial Mall South
  P.O. Box 94987
  Lincoln, NE 68509

Nevada

Supervisor of Teacher Certification
  State Department of Education
  400 West King Street
  Carson City, NV 89710

New Hampshire

Administrator of Teacher Education
    and Professional Standards
  State Department of Education
  101 Pleasant Street
  Concord, NH 03301

New Jersey

State of New Jersey
  Department of Education
  Teacher Certification and Academic Credentials
  3535 Quakerbridge Road
  CN 503
  Trenton, NJ 08625

New Mexico

Educator Preparation and Licensure
  New Mexico State Department of Education
  Santa Fe, NM 87503

New York

Division of Teacher Education and Certification
  Cultural Education Center
  Room 5A, 11
  Albany, NY 12230

North Carolina

Director, Division of Certification
  State Department of Public Instruction
  114 West Edenton Street
  Raleigh, NC 27611

North Dakota

Director of Teacher Certification
  State Department of Public Instruction
  Bismarck, ND 58505

Ohio

Director, Division of Teacher Education and Certification
    State Department of Education
    Columbus, OH 43215

Oklahoma

Administrator, Teacher Education and Certification
    State Department of Education
    2500 North Lincoln Boulevard
    Oklahoma City, OK 73105

Oregon

Teachers Standards and Practices Commission
    630 Center Street, NE
    Suite 200
    Salem, OR 97310

Pennsylvania

Pennsylvania Department of Education
    Bureau of Teacher Certification
    333 Market Street, 3d Floor
    Harrisburg, PA 17126

Puerto Rico

Teacher Certification Division
  Department of Education
  Box 759
  Hato Rey, PR 00919

Rhode Island

Coordinator for Teacher Education
  Certification and Placement
  State Department of Education
  Roger Williams Building
  22 Hayes Street
  Providence, RI 02908

South Carolina

Director of Teacher Education and Certification
  State Department of Education
  Rutledge Building, Room 1015
  Columbia, SC 29201

South Dakota

Director, Office of Teacher Education and Certification
  Division of Education
  Kneip Office Building
  700 Governors Drive
  Pierre, SD 57501

Tennessee

Director, Office of Teacher Licensing
  State Department of Education
  125 Cordell Hull Building
  Nashville, TN 37219

Texas

Director, Division of Teacher Certification
  Texas Education Agency
  1701 North Congress Avenue
  Austin, TX 78701

Utah

Supervisor of Teacher Certification
  Certification and Personnel Development
  Utah State Office of Education
  250 East Fifth Street
  Salt Lake City, UT 84111

Vermont

Director, Certification Division
  State Department of Education
  Montpelier, VT 05602

Virgin Islands

District Director
  Educational Personnel Services
  Department of Education
  44-46 Kongens Gade
  St. Thomas, Virgin Islands 00802

Virginia

Supervisor of Teacher Certification
  Division of Teacher Certification
  State Department of Education
  P.O. Box 6Q
  Richmond, VA 23216

Washington

Director of Certification and Licensing
  Office of the Superintendent of Public Instruction
  Old Capitol Building
  Olympia, WA 98504

West Virginia

Director, Office of Professional Education
  State Department of Education
  Capitol Complex, Room B-337
  Building 6
  Charleston, WV 25305

Wisconsin

Administrator, Teacher Certification
  Bureau of Teacher Education, Certification and
    Placement
  State Department of Public Instruction
  125 South Webster Street—P.O. Box 7841
  Madison, WI 53707

Wyoming

Director, Certification and Accreditation Services Unit
  State Department of Education
  Hathaway Building
  Cheyenne, WY 82202

OFFICES OF TEACHER CERTIFICATION IN CANADIAN PROVINCES AND TERRITORIES

Alberta

Alberta Education
  Communication Branch
  Devonian Building
  11160 Jasper Avenue
  Edmonton, AB T5K 0L2

British Columbia

Ministry of Education
  Parliament Buildings
  Victoria, BC V8V 2M4

Manitoba

Manitoba Administration and Professional
    Certification Branch
  #507, 1181 Portage Avenue
  Winnipeg, MB R3G 0T3

Newfoundland

Department of Education
  P.O. Box 8700
  St. John's, NF A1B 4J6

Northwest Territories

Department of Education, Cultures & Employment
  P.O. Box 1320
  Yellowknife, NT X1A 2L9

Nova Scotia

Department of Education
  Trade Mart
  P.O. Box 578
  Halifax, NS B3J 2S9

Ontario

Ministry of Education & Training
  14th Fl., Mowat Block, Queen's Park
  Toronto, ON M7A 1L2

Prince Edward Island

Department of Education
  P.O. Box 2000
  Charlottetown, PE C1A 7N8

Quebec

Ministere de l'Education
  Direction des communications 1035
  rue De La Chevrotiere, 11e etage,
  Quebec, PQ G1R 5A5

Saskatchewan

Saskatchewan Education Training & Employment
  2220 College Avenue
  Regina, SK S4P 3V7

Yukon Territory

Department of Education
  P.O. Box 2703
  Whitehorse, YT Y1A, 2C6

SELECTED PROFESSIONAL
JOURNALS IN THE SOCIAL SCIENCES

ANTHROPOLOGY

American Anthropologist
American Antiquity
American Ethnologist
American Journal of Archaeology
American Journal of Physical Anthropology
Anthropological Linguistics
Current Anthropology
Journal of Field Archaeolaogy

ECONOMICS

American Economist
Economic Journal
The Economist

International Journal of Social Economics
Journal of Cultural Economics
Journal of Economic Education
Journal of Environmental Economics and Management
Magazine of Wall Street
Review of Economic Studies
Review of Economics and Statistics
World Economic Monitor

GEOGRAPHY

American Congress on Surveying and Mapping Review
American Institute of Planners Journal
Environment and Planning
Geographical Journal
Journal of Cultural Geography
Journal of Geography
Journal of Travel Research
Research in Contemporary and Applied Geography
Urban Studies

HISTORY

American Archivist
American Historical Review
Current History

Historian: A Journal of History
Historic Preservation
The Historical Journal
The History Teacher
Journal of Popular Culture
Public Historian

POLITICAL SCIENCE

American Criminal Law Review
American Journal of Political Science
Journal of Politics
Modern Law and Society
Policy and Politics
Policy Studies Review
Political Science Quarterly
Proceedings of the Academy of Political Science
You and the Law
Your Business and the Law

PSYCHOLOGY

American Journal of Psychology
American Mental Health Counselors Journal
American Psychologist
Educational Psychologist

Journal of Applied Psychology
Journal of Consulting and Clinical Psychology
Journal of Cross-Cultural Psychology
Journal of Educational Psychology
Journal of Experimental Psychology
Journal of Psychology
Journal of School Psychology
Personnel and Guidance Journal
Psychology in the Schools

SOCIOLOGY

Aging
American Journal of Sociology
American Sociological Review
Gerontologist
Journal of Educational Sociology
Journal of Family Issues
Journal of Marriage and the Family
Rural Sociology
School and Society
Sociological Quarterly
Urban Life

APPENDIX D

SELECTED REFERENCES

Academic Preparation for College: What Students Need to Know and Be Able to Do. New York: The College Board, 1983.

Boyer, Ernest L. *High School: A Report on Secondary Education in America.* The Carnegie Foundation for the Advancement of Teaching. New York: Harper and Row, 1983.

Canadian Almanac and Directory. Toronto: Canadian Almanac and Directory, Ltd., 1996.

De Galan, Julie and Stephen Lambert. *Great Jobs for History Majors.* Lincolnwood, IL: VGM Career Horizons, 1995.

————. *Great Jobs for Psychology Majors.* Lincolnwood, IL: VGM Career Horizons, 1995.

Jackson, Kenneth, chair, The Bradley Commission on History in the Schools. *Building a History Curriculum.* Milwaukee: Bradley Foundation, 1988.

United States Department of Labor. *Occupational Outlook Handbook,* 1996–1997 edition. Lincolnwood, IL: VGM Career Horizons, 1996.

A complete list of titles in our extensive *Opportunities* series

OPPORTUNITIES IN

Accounting
Acting
Advertising
Aerospace
Agriculture
Airline
Animal & Pet Care
Architecture
Automotive Service
Banking
Beauty Culture
Biological Science
Biotechnology
Broadcasting
Building Construction Trades
Business Communications
Business Management
Cable Television
CAD/CAM
Carpentry
Chemistry
Child Care
Chiropractic
Civil Engineering
Cleaning Service
Commercial Art & Graphic
   Design
Computer Maintenance
Computer Science
Computer Systems
Counseling & Development
Crafts
Culinary
Customer Service
Data & Word Processing
Dental Care
Desktop Publishing
Direct Marketing
Drafting
Electrical Trades
Electronics
Energy
Engineering
Engineering Technology
Environmental
Eye Care
Farming and Agriculture
Fashion
Fast Food
Federal Government
Film
Financial
Fire Protection Services

Fitness
Food Service
Foreign Language
Forestry
Franchising
Funeral Services
Gerontology & Aging Services
Health & Medical
Heating, Ventilation, Air
   Conditioning, and
   Refrigeration
High Tech
Home Economics
Homecare Services
Horticulture
Hospital Administration
Hotel & Motel
Human Resources
   Management
Information Systems
Installation & Repair
Insurance
Interior Design & Decorating
International Business
Journalism
Laser Technology
Law
Law Enforcement &
   Criminal Justice
Library & Information
   Science
Machine Trades
Marine & Maritime
Marketing
Masonry
Medical Imaging
Medical Sales
Medical Technology
Mental Health
Metalworking
Military
Modeling
Music
Nonprofit Organizations
Nursing
Nutrition
Occupational Therapy
Office Occupations
Optometry
Paralegal
Paramedical
Part-Time & Summer Jobs
Performing Arts
Petroleum
Pharmacy

Photography
Physical Therapy
Physician
Physician Assistant
Plastics
Plumbing & Pipe Fitting
Postal Service
Printing
Property Management
Psychology
Public Health
Public Relations
Publishing
Purchasing
Real Estate
Recreation & Leisure
Religious Service
Research & Development
Restaurant
Retailing
Robotics
Sales
Science Technician
Secretarial
Social Science
Social Work
Special Education
Speech-Language Pathology
Sports & Athletics
Sports Medicine
State & Local Government
Teaching
Teaching English to Speakers
   of Other Languages
Technical Writing &
   Communications
Telecommunications
Telemarketing
Television & Video
Theatrical Design &
   Production
Tool & Die
Training & Development
Transportation
Travel
Trucking
Veterinary Medicine
Visual Arts
Vocational & Technical
Warehousing
Waste Management
Welding
Writing
Your Own Service Business

VGM Career Horizons
a division of *NTC/Contemporary Publishing Company*
4255 West Touhy Avenue
Lincolnwood, Illinois 60646–1975